Getting Started with Grunt JavaScript Task Runner

A hands-on approach to mastering the fundamentals of Grunt

Jaime Pillora

[PACKT] open source *
PUBLISHING
community experience distilled

BIRMINGHAM - MUMBAI

Getting Started with Grunt: The JavaScript Task Runner

Copyright © 2014 Packt Publishing

All rights reserved. No part of this book may be reproduced, stored in a retrieval system, or transmitted in any form or by any means, without the prior written permission of the publisher, except in the case of brief quotations embedded in critical articles or reviews.

Every effort has been made in the preparation of this book to ensure the accuracy of the information presented. However, the information contained in this book is sold without warranty, either express or implied. Neither the authors, nor Packt Publishing and its dealers and distributors, will be held liable for any damages caused or alleged to be caused directly or indirectly by this book.

Packt Publishing has endeavored to provide trademark information about all of the companies and products mentioned in this book by the appropriate use of capitals. However, Packt Publishing cannot guarantee the accuracy of this information.

First published: January 2014

Production Reference: 1170114

Published by Packt Publishing Ltd.
Livery Place
35 Livery Street
Birmingham B3 2PB, UK.

ISBN 978-1-78398-062-8

www.packtpub.com

The cover image is trademarked Bocoup LLC

Credits

Author
Jaime Pillora

Reviewers
Peter deHaan
Arnaud Tanielian

Acquisition Editors
Kartikey Pandey
Meeta Rajani

Lead Technical Editor
Sruthi Kutty

Technical Editors
Shashank Desai
Aman Preet Singh
Anand Singh

Project Coordinator
Aboli Ambardekar

Proofreader
Lauren Harkins

Indexer
Monica Ajmera Mehta

Production Coordinator
Alwin Roy

Cover Work
Alwin Roy

About the Author

Jaime Pillora is a passionate full-stack JavaScript developer, an open source advocate and contributor, and is currently the CTO of Luma Networks, a well-funded networking startup in Sydney, Australia.

Jaime has always been interested in all things computer science, and from a young age, he began to devote his time and effort to learning and perfecting his knowledge in the field. Jaime holds a Bachelor of Computer Science from the University of New South Wales. In all of his work, Jaime strives to reduce technical debt while maintaining maximum efficiency; this is done through software engineering best practices, combined with using the best tools for the given situation. Grunt is one such tool, which is utilized in every frontend project. Jaime's interest in Grunt began early on in his development career and he has since become a renowned expert.

Jaime has been working as a frontend JavaScript developer since 2008, and a backend JavaScript developer utilizing Node.js since 2011. Currently, Jaime leads all software development at Luma Networks, who is implementing software-defined networking on commodity hardware utilizing JavaScript.

> I would like to thank my loving partner, Jilarra, for her support during the many hours put into this book, and her contribution to the proofreading and editing of the final drafts.

About the Reviewers

Peter deHaan likes Grunt a lot and thinks it's the best thing to happen to Node.js since npm. You can follow his Grunt npm-twitter-bot feed at `@gruntweekly`.

Arnaud Tanielian is a happy French web developer who specializes in frontend projects such as FullJS, standards, HTML5, and GruntJS. He is a freelancer, traveling around the world and working from coffee shops to bars, currently living in Melbourne, Australia.

Look for `@Danetag` on the Internet and you'll find some cool projects, fun, and French clichés.

www.PacktPub.com

Support files, eBooks, discount offers and more

You might want to visit www.PacktPub.com for support files and downloads related to your book.

Did you know that Packt offers eBook versions of every book published, with PDF and ePub files available? You can upgrade to the eBook version at www.PacktPub.com and as a print book customer, you are entitled to a discount on the eBook copy. Get in touch with us at service@packtpub.com for more details.

At www.PacktPub.com, you can also read a collection of free technical articles, sign up for a range of free newsletters and receive exclusive discounts and offers on Packt books and eBooks.

http://PacktLib.PacktPub.com

Do you need instant solutions to your IT questions? PacktLib is Packt's online digital book library. Here, you can access, read and search across Packt's entire library of books.

Why Subscribe?
- Fully searchable across every book published by Packt
- Copy and paste, print and bookmark content
- On demand and accessible via web browser

Free Access for Packt account holders

If you have an account with Packt at www.PacktPub.com, you can use this to access PacktLib today and view nine entirely free books. Simply use your login credentials for immediate access.

Table of Contents

Preface	**1**
Chapter 1: Introducing Grunt	**7**
What is Grunt?	**7**
Why use Grunt?	**9**
Benefits of Grunt	**10**
Efficiency	10
Consistency	10
Effectiveness	11
Community	11
Flexibility	12
Real-world use cases	**13**
Static analysis or Linting	13
Transcompilation	16
CoffeeScript	16
Minification	**20**
Concatenation	**21**
Deployment	**23**
FTP	23
SFTP	25
S3	27
Summary	**28**
Chapter 2: Setting Up Grunt	**29**
Installation	**29**
Node.js	29
Modules	31
npm	33
Finding modules	35
Installing modules	35

Grunt	37
Project setup	**38**
package.json	39
Gruntfile.js	42
Directory structure	43
Configuring tasks	**44**
Configuring multitasks	47
Configuring options	48
Configuring files	49
Single set of source files	51
Multiple sets of source files	51
Mapping a source directory to destination directory	52
Templates	53
Summary	**54**
Chapter 3: Using Grunt	**55**
Creating your own tasks	**55**
Tasks	55
The task object	56
Task aliasing	57
Multitasks	58
The multitask object	60
Asynchronous tasks	61
Running tasks	**62**
Command-line	62
Task arguments	65
Runtime options	66
Task help	67
Programmatically	69
Automatically	70
Using third-party tasks	**72**
Searching for tasks	72
Official versus user tasks	72
Task popularity	73
Task features	73
Task stars	74
Summary	**74**
Chapter 4: Grunt in Action	**75**
Creating the build	**75**
Step 1 – initial directory setup	76
Step 2 – initial configuration	76
Step 3 – organizing our source files	81
Scripts	81

[ii]

Views	85
Styles	87
Step 4 – optimizing our build files	88
Scripts	89
Styles	90
Views	91
Step 5 – tasks and options	92
Step 6 – improving development flow	94
Step 7 – deploying our application	97
Summary	**99**
Chapter 5: Advanced Grunt	**101**
Testing with Grunt	**101**
Continuous integration with Grunt	**103**
External tasks	**103**
Grunt plugins	**104**
Useful plugins	108
JavaScript resources	**109**
Development tools	**110**
Author picks	110
Mac OS X	110
Sublime Text	111
SourceTree	111
Chrome DevTools	111
Community picks	111
WebStorm	111
Yeoman	112
Summary	**112**
Index	**113**

Preface

Getting Started with Grunt: The JavaScript Task Runner is an introduction to the popular JavaScript build tool, Grunt. This book aims to provide the reader with a practical skillset, which can be used to solve real-world problems. This book is example driven, so each feature covered in this book is explained and also reinforced through the use of *runnable* examples, this dual method of learning will provide the reader with the means to verify that the theory aligns with its practical use.

All of the software used in this book is open source and when covered, some will be accompanied with a short history while crediting the author. These open source developers do not release their work for monetary gain, instead, they hope to provide utility for others and to forward the community, and for this, they should be duly recognized.

What this book covers

Chapter 1, *Introducing Grunt*, explains exactly what Grunt is and why we would want to use it. Then, instead of starting at the very beginning, we temporarily jump ahead to review a set of real-world examples. This gives us a glimpse of what Grunt can do, which will help us to see how we could use Grunt in our current development workflow.

Chapter 2, *Setting Up Grunt*, after finishing our forward escapade, we jump back to the very beginning and start with the two primary technologies surrounding Grunt: Node.js and its package manager—npm. Then, we proceed to installing each of these tools and setting up our first Grunt environment. Next, we learn about the `package.json` and `Gruntfile.js` files and how they are used to configure a Grunt build. We will also cover the various Grunt methods used for configuration and the types of situations where each is useful.

Chapter 3, Using Grunt, extends on what we learned in the previous chapter, to the use and creation of tasks that consume our freshly made configuration. We will cover tasks, multitasks, and asynchronous tasks. We look in-depth into the task object and how we can use it effectively to perform common file-related actions. Finally, we review running Grunt tasks and methods that customize Grunt execution to our benefit.

Chapter 4, Grunt in Action, begins with an empty folder and gradually constructs a Grunt environment for a web application. Throughout this process, we use various examples from *Chapter 1, Introducing Grunt*, make use of the configuration strategies from *Chapter 2, Setting Up Grunt*, and include some extra features from *Chapter 3, Using Grunt*. At the end of this chapter, we shall be left with a Grunt environment that compiles and optimizes our CoffeeScript, Jade, and Stylus, and deploys our resulting web application to Amazon's S3.

Chapter 5, Advanced Grunt, introduces some of the more advanced use cases for Grunt; these introductions are intended to be purely an entry to each topic while providing the resources to learn more. We briefly cover testing with Grunt, Grunt plugins, advanced JavaScript, development tools and more.

What you need for this book

In order to run Grunt, you need an operating system capable of running Node.js; this includes Windows, Mac OS X, and certain flavors of Linux. You also need a command-line interface of some form; in Windows, you can use PowerShell or Command Prompt, and on Mac OS X and Linux, you will find a Terminal application available for use.

Who this book is for

The only requirement for this book is a basic understanding of JavaScript. The two most important JavaScript concepts to know are objects and functions. An understanding of how JavaScript Object Notation (JSON) data is structured is also required, however, this will follow naturally from learning JavaScript objects. From this starting point, you are able to enter the world of Grunt and begin to improve your development workflow.

If you are not familiar with JavaScript yet, *Code Academy* (http://gswg.io#code-academy) offers a fast and interactive introduction to the basics of JavaScript programming. If you have more time, *Marijn Haverbeke's Eloquent JavaScript* (http://gswg.io#eloquent-javascript) is a perfect book to give you a general understanding of what programming actually is, while focusing on JavaScript at the same time. In the free (Creative Commons License) HTML version of *Eloquent JavaScript*, Marijn uses the fact that you are reading the book in a Web Browser to his advantage by allowing you to run and edit the code examples right in the page. This interactive reading experience is extremely powerful, and I highly recommend *Eloquent JavaScript*.

Conventions

In this book, various font styles are used to differentiate between different types of information. Here are some examples of these styles, and an explanation of their meaning:

When referring to a short piece of information that relates to the code examples, like a variable or property name, or file or directory name, we'll use a light mono-space font:

"Based on this task, we notice that each `file` in the `files` array contains `src` and `dest` properties."

When referring to a large piece of information that relates to the code examples, like a portion of code, the contents of a file or the output from the command-line interface, we use black mono-space font:

```
grunt.initConfig({
  stringCheck: {
    file: './src/app.js',
    string: 'console.log('
  }
});
```

When referring to portion code in code, we note the example number and name at the top in a JavaScript comment (that is, text beginning with //).

When specifying user command line input among the command-line output, using Unix bash convention, we prepend a dollar symbol so we know what is input and what is output:

```
$ echo "hello world"
hello world
```

When referring to **new terms** and **important words**, we display them in bold.

When conveying a URL, we'll prefix the text with "http://" and use a mono-space font. This book's homepage (http://gswg.io/) is used as a URL shortener and as an intermediary in case URLs need to be updated. For example:

"For more information, see the Grunt Website at http://gswg.io#grunt."

Code examples

You can download the code examples for Getting Started with Grunt at http://gswg.io#examples. This URL will bring you to the Git repository housing the examples for this book. Here, you can find the instructions for downloading and running these examples. Once downloaded, you will find five folders, one for each chapter. Throughout this book, many code snippets begin with a JavaScript comment, referencing where that portion of code can be found within Code examples. For example, in *Chapter 2*, *Setting Up Grunt*, the first code snippet begins with //Code example 01-modules. Since we are currently reading *Chapter 2*, *Setting Up Grunt*, you will find the 01-modules example inside the gswg-examples/2/01-modules folder. If you are having problems running any of the examples or if you find a bug in any of the examples, please open an issue on Github here: http://gswg.io#examples-issues.

Reader feedback

Feedback from our readers is always welcome. Let us know what you think about this book—what you liked or may have disliked. Reader feedback is important for us to develop titles that you really get the most out of.

To send us general feedback, simply send an e-mail to feedback@packtpub.com, and mention the book title via the subject of your message.

If there is a topic in which you have expertise and you are interested in either writing or contributing to a book, see our author guide at http://www.packtpub.com/authors.

Customer support

Now you are the proud owner of a Packt book, we have a number of things to help you to get the most from your purchase.

Errata

Though we have taken every care to ensure the accuracy of our content, mistakes do happen. If you find a mistake in one of our books—maybe a mistake in the text or the code—we would be grateful if you would report this to us. By doing so, you can save other readers from frustration and help us improve subsequent versions of this book. If you find any errata, please report them by visiting http://www.packtpub.com/submit-errata, selecting your book, clicking on the **errata submission form** link, and entering the details of your errata. Once your errata are verified, your submission will be accepted and the errata will be uploaded on our website, or added to any list of existing errata, under the Errata section of that title. Any existing errata can be viewed by selecting your title from http://www.packtpub.com/support.

Piracy

Piracy of copyrighted material on the Internet is an ongoing problem across all media. At Packt, we take the protection of our copyright and licenses very seriously. If you come across any illegal copies of our works, in any form on the Internet, please provide us with the location address or website name immediately so that we can pursue a remedy.

Please contact us at copyright@packtpub.com with a link to the suspected pirated material.

We appreciate your help in protecting our authors and our ability to bring you valuable content.

Questions

You can contact us at questions@packtpub.com if you are having a problem with any aspect of the book, and we will do our best to address it.

Introducing Grunt

In this chapter, we will first define Grunt and cover some of the reasons why we would want to use it. Then, instead of starting at the beginning, we'll temporarily jump ahead to review some real-world use cases. Each example will contain a brief summary, but it won't be covered in detail, as the purpose is to provide a glimpse of what is to come. These examples will also provide us with a general understanding of what to expect from Grunt and hopefully, with this sneak peak, an idea of how Grunt's power and simplicity could be applied to our own projects.

What is Grunt?

When Ben Alman released Grunt (`http://gswg.io#grunt`) in March 2012, he described it as a task-based command line build tool for JavaScript projects. Now, with the release of Grunt version 0.4.x, the project caption is The JavaScript Task Runner. Build tools or task runners are most commonly used for automating repetitive tasks, though we will see that the benefits of using Grunt far exceed simple automation.

The terms build tool and task runner essentially mean the same thing and throughout this book, I will always use build tool, though both can be used interchangeably. Build tools are programs with the sole purpose of executing code to convert some source code into a final product, whether it be a complete web application, a small JavaScript library or even a Node.js command-line tool. This build process can be composed of any number of steps, including: style and coding practice enforcement, compiling, file watching and automatic task execution, and unit testing and end-to-end testing, just to name a few.

Introducing Grunt

Grunt has received huge success in the open-source community, especially with the rise of JavaScript following the world's increasing demand for web applications. At the time of writing this book (December 2013), Grunt is downloaded approximately 300,000 times per month (http://gswg.io#grunt-stats) and the open-source community has published approximately 1,400 Grunt plugins in npm (the Node.js package manager http://gswg.io#npm) and these numbers continue to rise.

Node.js (http://gswg.io#node) is a platform for writing JavaScript command-line tools, which run on all major operating systems. Grunt is one such command-line tool. Once installed, we can execute grunt on the command line. This tells Grunt to look for a Gruntfile.js file. This choice of name refers to the build tool **Make**, and its Makefile. This file is the entry point to our build, which can define tasks inline, load tasks from external files, load tasks from external modules, and configure these tasks and much more.

Let's briefly review a simple example of a Gruntfile.js file so we can get a glimpse of what is to come:

```
//Code example 01-minify
module.exports = function(grunt) {

  // Load the plugin that provides the "uglify" task.
  grunt.loadNpmTasks('grunt-contrib-uglify');

  // Project configuration.
  grunt.initConfig({
    uglify: {
      target1: {
        src: 'foo.js',
        dest: 'foo.min.js'
      }
    }
  });

  // Define the default task
  grunt.registerTask('default', ['uglify']);
};
```

In this short example, we are using the uglify plugin to create a minified (or compressed) version of our main project file—foo.js in this case. First, we load the plugin with loadNpmTasks. Next, we'll configure it by passing a configuration object to initConfig. Finally, we'll define a default task, which in this example, is simply an alias to the uglify task.

Now, we can run the `default` task with `grunt` and we should see the following output:

```
$ grunt
Running "uglify:target1" (uglify) task
File "foo.min.js" created.
Done, without errors.
```

We've just created and successfully run our first Grunt build!

Why use Grunt?

In the past five years, due to the evolution of Web browsers, focus has shifted from Desktop applications to Web applications. More companies are realizing that the web is a perfect platform to create tools to save people time and money by providing quick and easy access to their service. Whether it is ordering pizza or Internet banking, web applications are fast becoming the platform of choice for the modern business. These modern companies know that, if they were to build an application for a specific platform, like the iOS or Windows operating systems, they would be inherently restricting their audience, as each operating system has its own percentage of the total user base. They've realized that in order to reach *everyone*, they need a ubiquitous platform that exists in all operating systems. This platform is the Web. So, if everyone with Internet access has a browser, then by targeting the browser as our platform, our potential user base becomes everyone on the Internet.

The Google product line is a prime example of a business successfully utilizing the browser platform. This product line includes: Google Search, YouTube, Gmail, Google Drive, Google Docs, Google Calendar, and Google Maps. However, providing a rich user experience comes with a cost. These applications are tremendously more complex than a traditional website made with jQuery animated menus.

Complex JavaScript Web Applications require considerable design and planning. It is quite common for the client-side (or browser) JavaScript code to be more complicated than the server-side code. With this in mind, we need to ensure our code base is manageable and maintainable. The key to code manageability and maintainability is to *logically structure our project* and to *keep our code DRY*. Structuring includes the file and directory structure as well as the code structure (that is HTML, CSS, and JavaScript structure). Maintaining a logical directory structure provides predefined locations for all types of files. This allows us to always know where to put our code, which is very important for rapid development. DRY stands for Don't Repeat Yourself (http://gswg.io#dry). Hence, to keep your code DRY is to write code where there is little or no repetition and we embrace the idea of a "single source of truth". Similarly, we want to avoid repetition surrounding our build process. As we'll see throughout this book, Grunt is a great tool for achieving these goals.

Benefits of Grunt

Many people are of the opinion that the benefit of using Grunt (or any build tool for that matter) is to possibly save time, and often this tradeoff—of learning time versus actual development time is deemed too risky, which then leads to the programmer staying safe with the manual method. This perception is misguided. The added efficiency is only one of benefits of using Grunt, the other main benefits include: build consistency, increased effectiveness, community utilization, and task flexibility.

Efficiency

Hypothetically, let's say it takes us 2 minutes per build and we need to build (and run the tests) numerous times every hour, resulting in approximately 50 builds per day. With this schedule, it costs us approximately 100 minutes per day in order to perform the monotonous task of manual running various sets of command-line tools in the right sequence. Now, if learning a new build tool like Grunt takes us 2-3 hours of research and 1-2 hours to implement the existing build process as a Grunt build, then this cost will be recovered in only a week of work. Considering that most programmers will be using their trade for years to come, the decision is simple—use a build tool as it is well worth the time investment.

With this in mind, we can see the time spent to learn a new tool like Grunt is negligible in comparison with the time saved across the entire span of all projects in which that tool is used.

Consistency

The human propensity for error is an unavoidable hurdle programmers face when carrying out a manual build process. This propensity is further increased if a given build process involves each command being manually typed out instead of saving them in some kind of script for easier execution. Even with an array of scripts, problems can still arise if someone forgets to execute one, or if the special script required for a special situation is forgotten.

Using Grunt provides us with the ability to implement our build logic inside the build process. Once the build has been set up and confirmed, this effectively removes the possibility for human error from the equation entirely. This ability also helps newcomers contribute to your projects by allowing them to quickly get started on the code base as opposed to getting bogged down trying to understand the build.

Also, as a result of the great effort behind the Node.js project, we can also run our encapsulated build process across all major operating systems. This allows developers from all walks of life to use and enhance a common build process.

Effectiveness

As well as saving time from doing less, we also save time by staying in the zone. For many programmers, it often takes us some time to gather momentum in order to bring our brains into gear. By automating the build process, we multi-task less, allowing us to keep our minds focused on the current task at hand.

Community

A common problem for many build tools is the lack of community support. Most build tool have plugins for many common build processes, but as soon as we want to perform a task that is too niche or too advanced, we are likely to be forced to restart from scratch.

At the time of writing, npm (the Node.js Package Manager) contained approximately 50,000 modules and, as mentioned above, approximately 1,900 of these are Grunt plugins. These plugins cover a wide array of build problems and are available now via the public npm repository, which provides a purposefully simple means to publish new modules to the repository. As a result of this simplicity, anyone may share their Grunt plugin with the rest of the world with a single `npm publish` command. This concept makes it easy for programmers of every skill level to share their work. Allowing everyone to build upon everyone else's work creates a synergistic community, where the more people contribute, the more valuable the community becomes, which in turn provides further incentive for people to contribute. So, by using Grunt, we tap into the power of the Node.js community. This fact alone should be enough to convince us to use Grunt.

GitHub (`http://gswg.io#github`) is another valuable community tool that greatly benefits Grunt. As of June 2013, JavaScript code makes up 21 percent of code on GitHub making it the most popular programming language on GitHub. However, this fact alone is not the only reason to host your project on GitHub. The Git (`http://gswg.io#git`) **Distributed Version Control System** (**DVCS**) provides the ability to branch and merge code, and the flexibility of both local and remote repositories. This makes it the superior choice for open-source collaboration, compared to other (non-distributed) VCS tools such as SVN or TFS.

With the combination of GitHub (being a great JavaScript open-source collaboration platform) and npm (being so widespread and simple to use) the Grunt team provides Grunt users with the perfect environment for an open-source community to thrive.

We'll cover more on npm in the *Chapter 2, Setting Up Grunt* and contributing to open-source projects in *Chapter 5, Advanced Grunt*.

Introducing Grunt

Flexibility

Another common problem for many build tools is the level of prior knowledge required to write your own task. Often, they also require varying levels of setup before you can start actually writing code. A Grunt task is essentially just a JavaScript function, and that's it. Tasks can be defined with various levels of complexity to suit the needs of build process. However, remaining at the root of all tasks is the idea of one task being one function—for example, this `Gruntfile.js` defines a simple task called `foo`:

```
//Code example 02-simple-task
module.exports = function(grunt) {

  grunt.registerTask('foo', function() {
    grunt.log.writeln('foo is running...');
  });

};
```

Our new `foo` task is runnable with the command: `grunt foo`. When executed, we see:

```
$ grunt foo
Running "foo" task
foo is running...
```

We'll learn more about Grunt tasks in *Chapter 3, Using Grunt*.

The arguments for using various build tools generally stem from two conflicting sides: the simplicity of configuration or the power of scripting. With Grunt however, we get the best of both worlds. We are able to easily create arbitrary tasks as well as define verbose configuration. The following `Gruntfile.js` file demonstrates this:

```
//Code example 03-simple-config
module.exports = function(grunt) {

  grunt.initConfig({
    bar: {
      foo: 42
    }
  });

  grunt.registerTask('bar', function() {
    var bar = grunt.config.get('bar');
    var bazz = bar.foo + 7;
```

```
      grunt.log.writeln("Bazz is " + bazz);
    });
};
```

In this example, we are first initializing the configuration with an object. Then, we are registering a simple task, which uses this configuration. Note, instead of using `grunt.initConfig(...)` in the preceding code, we could also use `grunt.config.set('bar', { foo: 42 });` to achieve the same result.

When we run this example with `grunt bar`, we should see:

```
$ grunt bar
Running "bar" task
Bazz is 49
```

This example demonstrates the creation of a simple task using minimal configuration. Imagine we have created a task which parses JavaScript source code into a tree of syntax nodes, traverses these nodes, performing arbitrary transforms on them (like shortening variable names) and writes them back out to a file, with the ultimate effect of compressing our source code. This is exactly what the UglifyJS library does, with many configuration options to customize its operation. We'll cover more on *JavaScript Minification* in the next section.

Real-world use cases

Hearing about the benefits of Grunt is all well and good, but what about actual use cases that the average web developer will face every day in the real world? In this section, we'll take an eagle-eye view of the most common use cases for Grunt.

These examples make use of configuration targets. Essentially, targets allow us to define multiple configurations for a task. We'll cover more on configuration targets in *Chapter 2, Setting Up Grunt*.

Static analysis or Linting

In programming, the term **linting** is the process of finding *probable* bugs and/or style errors. Linting is more popular in dynamically typed languages as type errors may only be resolved at runtime. Douglas Crockford popularized JavaScript linting in 2011 with the release of his popular tool, JSLint.

JSLint is a JavaScript library, so it can be run in Node.js or in a browser. JSLint is a set of predetermined rules that enforce correct JavaScript coding practices. Some of these rules may be optionally turned on and off, however, many cannot be changed. A complete list of JSLint rules can be found at `http://gswg.io#jslint-options`.

Introducing Grunt

This leads us to JSHint. Due to Douglas Crockford's coding style being too strict for some, *Anton Kovalyov* has forked the JSLint project to create a similar, yet more lenient version, which he aptly named: JSHint.

I am a fan of *Douglas Crockford* and his book, *JavaScript – The Good Parts* (http://gswg.io#the-good-parts), but like Anton, I prefer a more merciful linter, so in this example below, we will use the Grunt plugin for JSHint: http://gswg.io#grunt-contrib-jshint.

```
//Code example 04-linting
//Gruntfile.js
module.exports = function(grunt) {

  // Load the plugin that provides the "jshint" task.
  grunt.loadNpmTasks('grunt-contrib-jshint');

  // Project configuration.
  grunt.initConfig({
    jshint: {
      options: {
        curly: true,
        eqeqeq: true
      },
      target1: ['Gruntfile.js', 'src/**/*.js']
    }
  });

  // Define the default task
  grunt.registerTask('default', ['jshint']);

};

//src/foo.js
if(7 == "7") alert(42);
```

In the preceding code, we first load the `jshint` task. We then configure JSHint to run on the `Gruntfile.js` file itself, as well as all of the `.js` files in the `src` directory and its subdirectories (which is `src/foo.js` in this case). We also set two JSHint options: `curly`, which ensures that curly braces are always used in `if`, `for`, and `while` statements; and `eqeqeq`, which ensures that strict equality `===` is always used.

JSHint has retained most of the optional rules from JSLint and it has also added many more. These rules can be found at: http://gswg.io#jshint-options.

Finally, we can run the `jshint` task with `grunt`, and we should see the following:

```
$ grunt
Running "jshint:target1" (jshint) task
Linting src/foo.js...ERROR
[L1:C6] W116: Expected '===' and instead saw '=='.
if(7 == "7") alert(42);
Linting src/foo.js...ERROR
[L1:C14] W116: Expected '{' and instead saw 'alert'.
if(7 == "7") alert(42);

Warning: Task "jshint:target1" failed. Use --force to continue.

Aborted due to warnings.
```

The result shows that JSHint found two warnings in the `src/foo.js` file on:

- Line 1, column 6 — since we've enforced the use of strict equality, `==` is not allowed, so it must be changed to `===`.
- Line 1, column 14 — since we've enforced the use of the curly braces, the `if` statement body must explicitly use curly braces.

Once we've fixed these two issues as follows:

```
if(7 === "7") {
  alert(42);
}
```

We can then re-run `grunt` and we should see:

```
$ grunt
Running "jshint:target1" (jshint) task
>> 2 files lint free.

Done, without errors.
```

Notice that two files were reported to be lint free. The second file was the `Gruntfile.js` file, and if we review this file, we see it does not break either of the two rules we enabled.

In summary, JSHint is very useful as the first step of our Grunt build as it can help catch simple errors, such as unused variables or accidental assignments in `if` statements. Also, by enforcing particular coding standards on the project's code base, it helps maintain code readability, as all code entering the shared repository will be normalized to a predetermined coding style.

Transcompilation

Transcompiling—also known as source-to-source compilation and often abbreviated to transpiling—is the process of converting the source code of one language to the source code of another. Within the web development community in recent years, there has been an increase in the use of transcompile languages such as Haml, Jade, Sass, LESS, Stylus, CoffeeScript, Dart, TypeScript, and more.

The idea of transcompiling has been around since the 1980s. A popular example was an original C++ compiler (Cfront) by Bjarne Stroustrup, which converted C++ (known as C with Classes at the time) to C.

CoffeeScript

CoffeeScript (http://gswg.io#coffeescript) is the most popular transpile language for JavaScript. It was released in 2009 by *Jeremy Ashkenas* and is now the 10th most popular language on GitHub with 3 percent of the all code in public Git repositories. Due to this popularity, a particularly common use case for the modern web developer is to compile CoffeeScript to JavaScript. This can be easily achieved with the Grunt plugin http://gswg.io#grunt-contrib-coffee.

In the following example, we'll use the `grunt-contrib-coffee` plugin to compile all of our CoffeeScript files:

```
//Code example 05-coffeescript
module.exports = function(grunt) {

  // Load the plugin that provides the "coffee" task.
  grunt.loadNpmTasks('grunt-contrib-coffee');

  // Project configuration.
  grunt.initConfig({
    coffee: {
      target1: {
        expand: true,
        flatten: true,
        cwd: 'src/',
        src: ['*.coffee'],
        dest: 'build/',
        ext: '.js'
      },
      target2: {
        files: {
          'build/bazz.js': 'src/*.coffee'
        }
```

```
            }
        }
    });

    // Define the default task
    grunt.registerTask('default', ['coffee']);
};
```

Inside the configuration, the `coffee` object has two properties; each of which defines a target. For instance, we might wish to have one target to compile the application source and another target to compile the unit test source. We'll cover more on tasks, multitasks, and targets in *Chapter 2, Setting Up Grunt*.

In this case, the `target1` target will compile each `.coffee` file in the `src` directory to a corresponding output file in the `build` directory. We can execute this target explicitly with `grunt coffee:target1`, which should produce the result:

```
$ grunt coffee:target1
Running "coffee:target1" (coffee) task
File build/bar.js created.
File build/foo.js created.

Done, without errors.
```

Next, `target2` will compile and combine each of the `.coffee` files in the `src` directory to a *single* file in the `build` directory called `bazz.js`. We can execute this target with `grunt coffee:target2`, which should produce the result:

```
grunt coffee:target2
Running "coffee:target2" (coffee) task
File build/bazz.js created.

Done, without errors.
```

Combining multiple files into one has advantages and disadvantages, which we shall review in the next section *Minification*.

Jade

Jade (`http://gswg.io#jade`) compiles to HTML and, as with CoffeeScript to JavaScript, Jade has the semantics of HTML, though different syntax. *TJ Holowaychuk*, an extremely prolific open-source contributor, released Jade in July 2010. More information on the Grunt plugin for Jade can be found at `http://gswg.io#grunt-contrib-jade`.

Introducing Grunt

We'll also notice the following example Gruntfile.js file is quite similar to the previous CoffeeScript example. As we will see with many Grunt plugins, both these examples define some kind of transform from one set of source files to another set of destination files:

```
//Code example 06-jade
module.exports = function(grunt) {

  // Load the plugin that provides the "jade" task.
  grunt.loadNpmTasks('grunt-contrib-jade');

  // Project configuration.
  grunt.initConfig({
    jade: {
      target1: {
        files: {
          "build/foo.html": "src/foo.jade",
          "build/bar.html": "src/bar.jade"
        }
      }
    }
  });

  // Define the default task
  grunt.registerTask('default', ['jade']);
};
```

In this example, target1 will do a one-to-one compilation, where src/foo.jade and src/bar.jade will be compiled into build/foo.html and build/bar.html respectively. As we have set the default task to be the jade task, we can run all of jade's targets with a simple grunt command, which should produce:

```
$ grunt
Running "jade:target1" (jade) task
File "build/foo.html" created.
File "build/bar.html" created.

Done, without errors.
```

Stylus

Stylus (http://gswg.io#stylus) compiles to CSS, and as before, it has the semantics of CSS though different syntax. *TJ Holowaychuk* also created Stylus, which he officially released in February 2011. More information on the Stylus Grunt plugin can be found at http://gswg.io#grunt-contrib-stylus. Similarly to the examples above, the following example `Gruntfile.js` file contains only slight differences. Instead of `jade`, we're configuring `stylus`, and instead of transpiling `.jade` to `.html`, we're transpiling `.styl` to `.css`:

```
//Code example 07-stylus
module.exports = function(grunt) {

  // Load the plugin that provides the "stylus" task.
  grunt.loadNpmTasks('grunt-contrib-stylus');

  // Project configuration.
  grunt.initConfig({
    stylus: {
      target1: {
        files: {
          "build/foo.css": "src/foo.styl"
        }
      }
    }
  });

  // Define the default task
  grunt.registerTask('default', ['stylus']);
};
```

When we run `grunt`, we should see the following:

```
$ grunt
Running "stylus:target1" (stylus) task
File build/foo.css created.

Done, without errors.
```

Haml, Sass, and LESS

Grunt plugins that transpile code are very similar, as previously seen with CoffeeScript, Jade and Stylus. In some way or another, they define a set of input files and a set of output files, and also provide options to vary the compilation. For the sake of brevity, I won't go through each one, but instead I'll provide links to each preprocessor (transcompiler tool) and its respective Grunt plugins:

- Haml—`http://gswg.io#haml—gswg.io#grunt-haml`
- Sass—`http://gswg.io#sass—gswg.io#grunt-contrib-sass`
- LESS—`http://gswg.io#less—gswg.io#grunt-contrib-less`

At the end of the day, the purpose of using transcompile languages is to improve our development workflow, not to hinder it. If using these tools requires a lengthy setup for each, then the more tools we add to our belt, the longer it'll take our team to get up and running. With Grunt, we add each plugin to our `package.json` and with one `npm install` command, we have all the plugins we need and can start transpiling in minutes!

Minification

As web applications increase in complexity, they also increase in size. They contain more HTML, more CSS, more images, and more JavaScript. To provide some context, the uncompressed development version of the popular JavaScript library, jQuery (v1.9.1), has reached a whopping 292 KB. With the shift to mobile, our users are often on unreliable connections and loading this uncompressed jQuery file could easily take more than 5 seconds. This is only one file, however, often websites can be as large as 2-3MB causing load times to skyrocket. A blog post from KISSmetrics (`http://gswg.io#loading-time-study`) reveals the following, using data from `gomez.com` and `akamai.com`:

> *73% of mobile Internet users say they have encountered a website that was too slow to load.*
>
> *51% of mobile Internet users say they have encountered a website that crashed, froze, or received an error.*
>
> *38% of mobile Internet users say they have encountered a website that wasn't available.*
>
> *47% of consumers expect a web page to load in 2 seconds or less.*
>
> *40% of people abandon a website that takes more than 3 seconds to load.*

A 1 second delay in page response can result in a 7% reduction in conversions.

If an e-commerce site is making $100,000 per day, a 1 second page delay could potentially cost you $2.5 million in lost sales every year.

Based on this information, it is clear we should do all we can to reduce page load times. However, manually minifying all of our assets is time consuming, so it is Grunt to the rescue! The Grunt team has plugins for the following common tasks:

- Minify JavaScript—`http://gswg.io#grunt-contrib-uglify`
- Minify CSS—`http://gswg.io#grunt-contrib-cssmin`
- Minify HTML—`http://gswg.io#grunt-contrib-htmlmin`

In the following example `Gruntfile.js`, we see how easy this process is. Much like the compilation tasks above, these minification tasks are also a transformation, in that they have file inputs and file outputs. In this example, we'll utilize the `grunt-contrib-uglify` plugin, which will provide the `uglify` task:

```
grunt.initConfig({
  uglify: {
    target1: {
      src: 'foo.js',
      dest: 'foo.min.js'
    }
  }
});
```

This is only a portion of `Code example 01-minify`, the complete snippet can be found in the code examples (`http://gswg.io#examples`) or by returning to the start of this chapter. As with the `uglify` task, the `cssmin` and `htmlmin` tasks also have options to customize the way our code is compressed. See the corresponding GitHub project pages for more information.

> If you're using Jade to construct your HTML, then you can use its built-in compression option by setting `pretty` to `false`.

Concatenation

As with minification, concatenation (or joining) also helps reduce page load time. As per the HTTP 1.1 specification, browsers can only request two files at once (see HTTP 1.1 Pipelining). Although newer browsers have broken this rule and will attempt to load up to six files at once, we will see it is still the cause of slower page load times.

Introducing Grunt

For example, if we open Chrome Developer Tools inside Google Chrome, view the Network tab, then visit the `cnn.com` website, we see approximately 120 file requests, 40 of which are loading from the `cnn.com` domain. Hence, even with six files being loaded at once, our browsers still must wait until a slot opens up before they can start downloading the next set of files.

Also, if there are more files to load over a longer period of time, there will be a higher chance of TCP connection dropouts, resulting in even longer waits. This is due to the browser being forced to re-establish a connection with the server.

When building a large Web Application, JavaScript will be used heavily. Often, without the use of concatenation, developers decide not to segregate their code into discrete modular files, as they would then be required to enter a corresponding script tag in the HTML. If we know all of our files will be joined at build-time, we will be more liberal with creation of new files, which in turn will guide us toward a more logical separation of application scope.

Therefore, by concatenating assets of similar type together, we can reduce our asset count, thereby increasing our browser's asset loading capability.

Although concatenation was solved decades ago with the Unix command: `cat`, we won't use `cat` in this example, instead, we'll use the Grunt plugin: http://gswg.io#grunt-contrib-concat. This example `Gruntfile.js` file demonstrates use of the `concat` task, which we'll see is very similar to the tasks above as it is also a fairly simple transformation:

```
//Code example 08-concatenate
module.exports = function(grunt) {

  // Load the plugin that provides the "concat" task.
  grunt.loadNpmTasks('grunt-contrib-concat');

  // Project configuration.
  grunt.initConfig({
    concat: {
      target1: {
        files: {
          "build/abc.js": ["src/a.js", "src/b.js", "src/c.js"]
        }
      }
    }
  });

  // Define the default task
```

```
    grunt.registerTask('default', ['concat']);
};
```

As usual, we will run it with `grunt` and should see the following:

```
$ grunt
Running "concat:target1" (concat) task
File "build/abc.js" created.

Done, without errors.
```

Just like that, our three source files have been combined into one, in the order we specified.

Deployment

Deployment is one of the lengthier tasks when it comes to releasing the final product. Generally, it involves logging into a remote server, manually finding the correct files to copy, restarting the server and praying we didn't forget anything. There may also be other steps involved which could further complicate this process, such as performing a backup of the current version or modifying a remote configuration file. Each one of these steps can be catered for with Grunt, either with plugins, which provide useful tasks, or with our own custom tasks where we may wield the complete power of Node.js.

As mentioned in the first section, we can use Grunt to script these types of processes, thus removing the element of human error. Human error is probably the most dangerous at the deployment step because it can easily result in server down time, which will often result in monetary losses.

In the following subsections, we'll cover three common methods of deploying files to our production servers: FTP, SFTP, and S3. We won't however, cover the creation of custom tasks and plugins in this section, as we will go through these topics in depth in *Chapter 3, Using Grunt*.

FTP

The File Transfer Protocol specification was released in 1980. Because of FTP's maturity and supremacy, FTP became the standard way to transfer files across the Internet. Since FTP operates over a TCP connection, and given the fact that Node.js excels in building fast network applications, an FTP client has been implemented in JavaScript in approximately 1000 lines, which is tiny! It can be found at `http://gswg.io#jsftp`.

A Grunt plugin has been made using this implementation, and this plugin can be found at http://gswg.io#grunt-ftp-deploy. In the following example, we'll use this plugin along with a local FTP server:

```
//Code example 09-ftp
module.exports = function(grunt) {

  // Load the plugin that provides the "ftp-deploy" task.
  grunt.loadNpmTasks('grunt-ftp-deploy');

  // Project configuration.
  grunt.initConfig({
    'ftp-deploy': {
      target1: {
        auth: {
          host: 'localhost',
          port: 21,
          authKey: 'my-key'
        },
        src: 'build',
        dest: 'build'
      }
    }
  });
  // Define the default task
  grunt.registerTask('default', ['ftp-deploy']);
};
```

When the ftp-deploy task is run, it looks for an .ftppass file, which contains sets of usernames and passwords. When placing a Grunt environment inside a version control system, we must be wary of unauthorized access to login credentials. Therefore, it is good practice to place these credentials in an external file, which is not under version control. We could also use system environment variables to achieve the same effect.

Our Gruntfile.js above has set the key option to "my-key", this tells ftp-deploy to look for this property inside our .ftppass file (which is in JSON format). So, we should create a .ftppass file like:

```
{
  "my-key": {
    "username": "john",
    "password": "smith"
  }
}
```

> For testing purposes, there are free FTP servers available: PureFTPd
> `http://gswg.io#pureftpd` (Mac OS X) and FileZilla Server
> `http://gswg.io#filezilla-server` (Windows).

Once we have an FTP server ready, with the correct username and password, we are ready to transfer. Running this example should produce the following:

```
$ grunt
Running "ftp-deploy:target1" (ftp-deploy) task
>> New remote folder created /build/
>> Uploaded file: foo.js to: /
>> FTP upload done!
```

FTP is widespread and commonly supported; however, as technology and software improve, as legacy systems get deprecated, and as data encryption becomes a negligible computational cost, the use of unencrypted protocols like FTP is in decline—which segues us to SFTP.

SFTP

The Secure File Transfer Protocol is often incorrectly assumed to be a normal FTP connection tunneled through an SSH (Secure Shell) connection. However, SFTP is a new file transfer protocol (though it does use SSH).

In this example, we are copying three HTML files from our local `build` directory to the remote `tmp` directory. Again, to avoid placing credentials inside `build`, we store our `username` and `password` inside our `credentials.json` file. This example uses the Grunt plugin `http://gswg.io#grunt-ssh`. This plugin actually provides two tasks: `sftp` and `sshexec`, however, in this example we'll only be using the `sftp` task:

```
//Code example 10-sftp
module.exports = function(grunt) {

  // Load the plugin that provides the "sftp" task.
  grunt.loadNpmTasks('grunt-ssh');

  // Project configuration.
  grunt.initConfig({

    credentials: grunt.file.readJSON('credentials.json'),

    sftp: {
      options: {
        host: 'localhost',
```

Introducing Grunt

```
            username: '<%= credentials.username %>',
            password: '<%= credentials.password %>',
            path: '/tmp/',
            srcBasePath: 'build/'
         },
         target1: {
            src: 'build/{foo,bar,bazz}.html'
         }
      }
   });

   // Define the default task
   grunt.registerTask('default', ['sftp']);
};
```

At the top of our configuration, we created a new `credentials` property to store the result of reading our `credentials.json` file. Using Grunt templates, which we cover in *Chapter 2, Setting Up Grunt*, we can list the path to the property we wish to substitute in. Once we have prepared our `credentials.json` file, we can execute grunt:

```
$ grunt
Running "sftp:target1" (sftp) task

Done, without errors.
```

We notice the `sftp` task didn't display any detailed information. However, if we run Grunt with the verbose flag: `grunt -v` we should see this snippet at the end of our output:

```
Connection :: connect
copying build/bar.html to /tmp/bar.html
copied build/bar.html to /tmp/bar.html
copying build/bazz.html to /tmp/bazz.html
copied build/bazz.html to /tmp/bazz.html
copying build/foo.html to /tmp/foo.html
copied build/foo.html to /tmp/foo.html
Connection :: end
Connection :: close

Done, without errors.
```

This output clearly conveys that we have indeed successfully copied our three HTML files from our local directory to the remote directory.

S3

Amazon Web Service's Simple Storage Service is not a deployment method (or protocol) like FTP and SFTP, but rather a service. Nevertheless, from a deployment perspective they are quite similar as they all require some configuration, including destination and authentication information.

Hosting Web Applications in the Amazon Cloud has grown quite popular in recent years. The relatively low prices of S3 make it a good choice for static file hosting, especially as running your own servers can introduce many unexpected costs. AWS has released a Node.js client library for many of its services. Since there was no Grunt plugins utilizing this library at the time, I decided to make one. So, in the following example, we are using http://gswg.io#grunt-aws. Below, we are attempting to upload all of the files inside the build directory into the root of the chosen bucket:

```
//Code example 11-aws
grunt.initConfig({
  aws: grunt.file.readJSON("credentials.json"),
  s3: {
    options: {
      accessKeyId: "<%= aws.accessKeyId %>",
      secretAccessKey: "<%= aws.secretAccessKey %>",
      bucket: "..."
    },
    //upload all files within build/ to output/
    build: {
      cwd: "build/",
      src: "**"
    }
  }
});
```

Again, similar to the SFTP, we are using an external credentials.json file to house our valuable information. So, before we can run this example, we first need to create a credentials.json file, which looks like:

```
{
  "accessKeyId": "AKIAIMK...",
  "secretAccessKey": "bt5ozy7nP9Fl9..."
}
```

Next, we set the `bucket` option to the name of bucket we wish to upload to, then we can go ahead and execute `grunt`:

```
$ grunt
Running "s3:build" (s3) task
Retrieving list of existing objects...
>> Put 'foo.html'
>> Put 'bar.js'
>> Put 2 files

Done, without errors.
```

Summary

In this chapter, we have learnt Grunt is an easy to use JavaScript build tool, which has the potential to greatly improve the development cycle of the typical front-end developer. We have covered many common build problems in this chapter and, by combining these examples, we see we can quite easily make use of various premade Grunt plugins to vastly simplify previously complex build processes.

In the next chapter, we will review the steps required to install Grunt and its only dependency—Node.js, and also the various methods of configuring Grunt.

2
Setting Up Grunt

In this chapter, we will go over the steps required to get Grunt up and running. We begin with an introduction into Node.js and npm, as they are the key technologies used to build the foundations upon which Grunt stands. We review Node.js modules and how they relate to Grunt, then cover the basics of a Grunt environment, including `package.json` and `Gruntfile.js` files. Once we are set up, we'll move onto configuring Grunt. We will look into the various methods and strategies that make Grunt best convey our build.

Installation

In this section, we cover how to install and use Grunt's key components, Node.js and npm. We will review a brief introduction into each, as well as their core concepts. Subsequently, we will cover the simple installation of Grunt itself.

Node.js

Although this book primarily focuses on Grunt, we will also dip our toes into the world of Node.js (http://gswg.io#node) fairly regularly. Given Grunt is written as a Node.js module and Grunt tasks and plugins are also Node.js modules, it is important that we understand the basics of Node.js and its package manager, npm (http://gswg.io#npm).

Ryan Dahl started the Node.js project in early 2009 out of frustration with the current state of web servers in the industry. At the time, web servers written in Ruby (Mongrel and then Thin) were popular due to the Ruby on Rails framework. Ryan realized that writing a really fast web server in Ruby just wasn't possible. Ruby's inefficiency was actually caused by the language's blocking nature, which meant – in context of a web server – that it could not effectively use the hardware available to it. A program is said to be blocking when it causes the CPU to be put on pause while it waits on a given **Input/Output (I/O)** task such as reading from the hard drive or making a network request to a web server.

Blocking is inherent in many programming languages. JavaScript and hence Node.js can avoid the blocking problem through its evented execution model. This model allows JavaScript programs to execute code asynchronously. That is, I/O tasks within JavaScript programs can be written so they don't block, and therefore achieve a high degree of efficiency.

The following table from Ryan Dahl's original Node.js presentation (http://gswg.io#node-presentation) in late 2009 shows the main types of I/O operations and using the average access time, the corresponding number of CPU cycles that could have been used during each I/O operation:

I/O operation	CPU cycles
L1	3 cycles
L2	14 cycles
RAM	250 cycles
Disk	41,000,000 cycles
Network	240,000,000 cycles

Based on this table, by blocking the CPU on any disk or network access, we are introducing large inefficiencies into our programs; so using Node.js is a huge step forward when building any application dealing with system I/O – which is most applications today.

On a general note, learning how the language works, where it excels and where it doesn't, and why JavaScript isn't the "toy" language that many have previously labeled it, will be of great value when traversing the JavaScript landscape. For a list of useful JavaScript resources, see *Chapter 5, Advanced Grunt*.

To install Node.js, first we visit the Node.js download page: http://gswg.io#node-download. Once there, you should see the following table of download options:

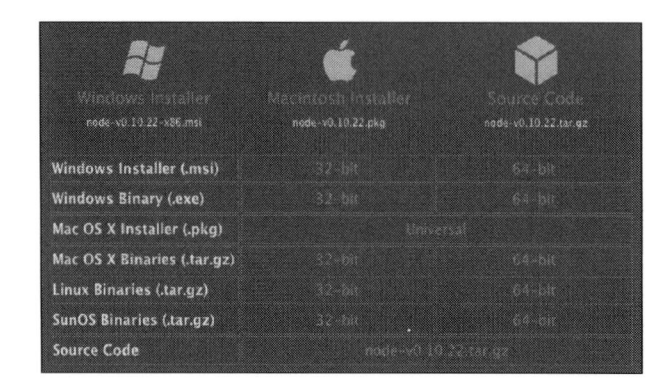

At the time of writing, the newest Node.js version is 0.10.22. This will most likely change, but fear not! The download page always contains the latest stable release of Node.js.

On Windows and Mac, the installers are the simplest way of installing Node.js. However, some may prefer using an operating system package manager, as they generally provide a more uniform method to install, uninstall, and most importantly – upgrade. For instance, if you are on a Mac, using homebrew to install Node.js is also very simple and it provides the added benefit of easy version upgrades to new versions as they're released, with the command: `brew upgrade node`. To read more on installing Node.js via a package manager, see `http://gswg.io#node-with-package-manager`. This page contains installation guides for Mac, Windows, Ubuntu, and various other Linux distributions. We'll learn more about homebrew in *Chapter 5, Advanced Grunt*, in the Development tools section.

Now we have installed Node.js, which has npm bundled along with it; we should have access to the `node` and `npm` executables, as they should now reside in our system's PATH.

The following commands should print the version of each executable to the console: `node --version` and `npm --version`, which should display the Node.js version that you just downloaded and installed. At the time of writing, my output looks like:

```
$ node --version
v0.10.22
$ npm --version
1.3.14
```

This confirms that we have set up Node.js correctly, and we are now ready to use it!

Modules

Before we look at npm, we first need to understand the basics of the Node.js module system. The Node.js module system is an implementation of the **CommonJS** specification. CommonJS describes a simple syntax for JavaScript programs to require (or import) other JavaScript programs into their context. This missing feature of JavaScript greatly assists with creating modular systems by simplifying the process of separating concerns. In Node.js, all JavaScript files can be seen as individual modules. So, beyond this point, we'll use the terms: file and module interchangeably. We may have also heard the term package being used in the place of module, which can be confusing. Rest assured, however, we'll cover packages in the next section on npm.

Setting Up Grunt

The CommonJS 1.1.1 specification can be found at http://gswg.io#commonjs. This specification describes the use of the following variables:

- module – an object representing the module itself. The module object contains the exports object. In the case of Node.js, it also contains meta-information, such as id, parent, and children.
- exports – a plain JavaScript object, which may be augmented to expose functionality to other modules. The exports object is returned as the result of a call to require.
- require – a function is used to import modules, returning the corresponding exports object.

In the case of Node.js, modules can be imported by filename using relative paths or absolute paths. When using npm (which stores modules in the node_modules directory), modules can also be imported by module name, which we'll see more on in the next subsection. In the case of a web browser, another implementation of CommonJS might require modules by URL.

The CommonJS specification also contains the following sample code, slightly modified for the purpose of clarity:

```
//Code example 01-modules
//program.js
var inc = require('./increment').increment;
var a = 1;
console.log(inc(a));

//increment.js
var add = require('./math').add;
exports.increment = function(b) {
    return add(b, 1);
};

//math.js
exports.add = function(c, d) {
    return c + d;
};
```

In this example, we'll use program.js as our entry point or "main" file. Since we know require will return the exports object of the desired file, it's quite easy to see what it does. Starting at program.js, we can see that it calls require('./increment'). When this require function is called, it synchronously executes the increment.js file. The increment.js module in turn, calls require('./math'). The math.js file augments its exports object with an add function.

Once the `math.js` file completes execution, `require` returns the `math.js` module's `exports` object, thereby allowing `increment.js` to use the `add` function. Subsequently, `increment.js` will complete its execution and return its `exports` object to `program.js`. Finally, `program.js` uses its new `inc` function to increment the variable a from 1 to 2. Now, when we run `program.js` with Node.js, we should see the following result:

```
$ node program.js
2
```

The important takeaway from this example is the separation of concerns provided by this modularity. Notice that the `program.js` module has no notion of the `add.js` module, yet it is doing most of the work. In computer science, the idea of abstracting functionality is not a new one; and with Node.js implementing CommonJS, it has provided a simple way for users to write modular programs in JavaScript. We could place this functionality in a single file, but if we were to extend `math.js` to include every common math function, its size and complexity would quickly grow. By splitting modules into submodules, we are separating the concerns of our program, transforming it from a single large complex program into multiple small and simple programs. The idea of many small programs working together is one of the foundations of Node.js. This helps us steer clear of large monolithic libraries such as jQuery v1.x.x, making their way into Node.js. Libraries of that size would be split up into smaller modules, allowing the user to use only what they require. The official documentation of the Node.js module system can be found at `http://gswg.io#node-modules`.

npm

As previously noted, npm is the Node.js package manager. Since the release of Node.js version 0.6.3, npm comes prepackaged with each Node.js distribution. npm provides the means to publish Node.js packages into the npm repository under a unique name. Subsequently, such a package may be installed by anyone who knows this unique name. This is the essence of npm – sharing and retrieving code from a public repository. "What is a package?" we may ask. On the npm **Frequently Asked Questions (FAQ)** page (`http://gswg.io#npm-what-is-a-package`), we see the following extract:

> *"What is a package?*
>
> *A package is:*
>
> *a) a folder containing a program described by a* `package.json` *file*
>
> *b) a gzipped tarball containing (a)*
>
> *c) a url that resolves to (b)"*

Points d) through g) have been removed for brevity, however each definition results in a). So ultimately, a package is any folder containing a valid `package.json` file. This is the only requirement to pass as an npm package.

In the last part we learned about modules, while relating back to the CommonJS specification. With the introduction of npm, there was a need to extend the CommonJS definition. The following description of a module is outlined on the npm FAQ page (http://gswg.io#npm-what-is-a-module):

> *"What is a module?*
>
> *A module is anything that can be loaded with* `require()` *in a Node.js program. The following things are all examples of things that can be loaded as modules:*
>
> *A folder with a* `package.json` *file containing a* `main` *field.*
>
> *A folder with an* `index.js` *file in it.*
>
> *A JavaScript file."*

So, as well as being a single JavaScript file, a module can be any folder with an `index.js` file in it, and can be any folder with a `package.json` file containing a main field (basically, the main field allows us to rename `index.js`). Notice that these two new definitions approximately coincide with the definition of a package. A package is folder that has a `package.json` file and a module can be a folder with `package.json` file or an `index.js` file. So, in order for someone to use your package in their program, it must be loaded with the `require` function, which by definition, means your package must also be a module. This is why Node.js programs are commonly referred to as "node modules" not "node packages" because "module" is more fitting in most scenarios.

In the early years, soon after Node.js v0.1.8 was released, the platform started with only the CommonJS-based module system outlined in the past section. It had no sanctioned way to find and publish modules. Isaac Schlueter saw this gap and set out to fill it, starting the npm project in September 2009. In early 2010, Ryan requested Isaac to join him at Joyent to work on npm and Node.js full-time. In January 2012, Ryan stepped down as the "gatekeeper" of the Node.js project and handed over the reins to Isaac.

A fun fact is that many believe they bring the truth when they quote "npm is not an acronym for the **Node Package Manager**" from the npm FAQ. However, Isaac was being humorous on the day of writing and this is not actually true. As some might say, he was "trolling".

npm has a many features, though for purposes of this book, we'll cover the two most relevant workflows: finding modules and installing modules.

Finding modules

The search feature of npm is fairly straightforward; we type the command `npm search` followed by the search terms we wish to match. If we were to enter: `npm search grunt concat`, npm would return all packages which match both `grunt` and `concat`. A term is considered a match if it's contained anywhere in the title, description, tags, or dependencies of the package descriptor, that is, the `package.json` file. So, before we use Google to find modules, it's best to try `npm search` first, as npm will search through metadata that does not appear on the npm website and is hence not indexed by Google. Let's say we wanted to find a Grunt plugin that makes use of the Unix `rsync` tool. We might try `npm search gruntplugin rsync`. In this case we've included `gruntplugin`, which according to the Grunt team, is a recommended tag for all Grunt plugins to use. We have also included `rsync`, to narrow the search down to only those Grunt plugins matching `rsync`. This command currently yields:

```
$ npm search gruntplugin rsync
```

NAME	DESCRIPTION
grunt-rsync	A Grunt task for accessing the file copying and syncing capabilities of the
grunt-rsync-2	Copy files to a (remote) machine with rsync. supports maps with target:source

Once we've found a potentially useful package, we can view its package information with `npm info <name>`, so we use `npm info grunt-rsync` in this case. However, in most cases, we just want to know how to use it. So, if the package has a public Git repository and also adheres to open source best practice, it should have a README file documenting its usage. We can open this repository page with the `npm repo <name>` command. Now that we've read about the package and we've decided that it may be what we're searching for, it is time to install it.

Installing modules

The `npm install` command has one purpose: to download modules from the npm repository. When installing a module, we can either install it locally or globally. We would choose to install a module locally if we're to use it in another module or application, and we'd choose a global install if we wanted to use the module as a command-line tool.

Setting Up Grunt

When we installed Node.js, a folder for npm "binaries" files was created and added to your system's PATH. This allows npm to globally install modules by placing a symbolic link in this directory, which points to the file specified in the `package.json` file's `bin` field. We say "binaries" here as the term binary file generally means some kind of compiled machine code; however, in this case, an npm binary is simply a JavaScript file. For example, if we wanted to install the `express` module globally, we would use the command: `npm install -g express`.

In the context of Grunt, we'll mainly be using `npm install` to utilize plugins locally inside a specific Grunt environment. Let's say we are developing a jQuery plugin and we wish to minify our source code. We can achieve this with the `grunt-contrib-uglify` plugin. In order to use this plugin in our `Gruntfile.js` file, we must first install it locally with the command: `npm install grunt-contrib-uglify`. This will place the newly downloaded module inside the current package's `node_modules` folder. To determine the current package, npm will traverse up the file directory tree from the current working directory, looking a module descriptor – `package.json`. If a `package.json` file is found, its containing folder will be used as the package root directory; however, if it is not found, the npm will assume there is no package yet and use the current directory as the package root directory. Once a package root directory has been determined, a `node_modules` folder will be created (if one doesn't already exist) and then finally, the module we're installing will be placed in there. To help solidify this, consider the following directory structure:

```
//Code example 02-npm-install-directory
└── project
    ├── a
    │   └── b
    │       └── c
    │           └── important.js
    └── package.json
```

If we run `npm install grunt-contrib-uglify` from the c directory, the project directory will be used as the package root directory, as it contains `package.json`.

`$ cd project/a/b/c`

`$ npm install grunt-contrib-uglify`

Once complete, the preceding command will result in the following directory structure:

```
└── project
    ├── a
    │   └── b
    │       └── c
    │           └── important.js
```

```
├── node_modules
│   ├── grunt-contrib-uglify
│   │   └── ...
│   └── ...
└── package.json
```

However, if we removed `package.json` before npm installing this same command would instead result in the following directory structure:

```
└── project
    └── a
        └── b
            └── c
                ├── important.js
                └── node_modules
                    ├── grunt-contrib-uglify
                    │   └── ...
                    └── ...
```

This pattern of calculating where to place the `node_modules` directory is compatible with the pattern that the `require` function uses to find modules. When we wish to use a newly installed module, we call the `require` function with the module's name (instead of a filename). The `require` function will look for the `node_modules` folder in the current directory and if it's not there, it will check the parent directory. It will keep searching up the directory tree until it finds a `node_modules` folder or until it reaches the root of the drive. Therefore, we can always require a module from where it was installed, even if it was actually placed many folders up the directory tree.

Now that we've installed `grunt-contrib-uglify`, we can load this module's Grunt tasks using: `grunt.loadNpmTasks("grunt-contrib-uglify")` within our `Gruntfile.js` file. The `loadNpmTasks` function searches for our `node_modules` folder in a similar way the `require` function. Once found it will look inside for the desired module. Lastly, it will load all of the files in the module's `tasks` directory. This is how a single module (a Grunt plugin) can provide multiple tasks.

Grunt

Finally, we can install Grunt! The Grunt **Command-line interface** (CLI) is published as a separate module for one important reason: to allow us to work on one machine, on multiple projects with various backward-incompatible versions of Grunt, without concern. We can do this because the `grunt-cli` module searches for an instance of Grunt (the `grunt` module) within the current directory or its parent directories (again, similar to the `require` function).

Setting Up Grunt

This means we can pull a legacy Grunt project (v0.3.x) and run `grunt` on the command line (which is actually the `grunt-cli` module). Then, navigate to a different Grunt project (v0.4.x) and run `grunt` again; both will run seamlessly. With this in mind, we should be able to see why we install `grunt-cli` globally and `grunt` locally.

First, we'll install `grunt-cli` with the following command:

```
$ npm install -g grunt-cli
```

> It should be noted that on Mac and Linux, we might receive a permissions error when installing modules globally. To remedy this we can prepend `sudo`, for example, `sudo npm install -g grunt`. However, modules are able to execute arbitrary code on installation; therefore, using `sudo` may be considered unsafe. To prevent this, it's best to reinstall Node.js without using `sudo`. For more information on this topic, please see this GitHub Gist (http://gswg.io#npm-no-sudo) by Isaac Schlueter.

Next, we'll find the project in which we wish to use Grunt and we'll use the following command:

```
$ cd my-project/
$ npm install grunt
```

Note, however that when it becomes time to set up this particular project again, we would prefer not to have to manually remember every module we used. One solution to this problem is to save our `node_modules` folder along with our project. This might be okay in some cases, however, npm was built to house and serve modules. In this next section, we'll see a better solution using npm, our `package.json` file and the `dependencies` field.

Project setup

Now we have installed Node.js, npm and Grunt, we're ready to create our first Grunt environment. Let's say we've already built a website, now we want to use Grunt to minify our assets. In this section, we'll learn about the two required files: the `package.json` file and the `Gruntfile.js` file, as well as a recommended directory structure.

package.json

The `package.json` file is a package descriptor; it is used to store all metadata about the module, such as name, version, description, author, repository, and more. It's the single file required to effectively use npm, therefore, the `package.json` file can also be thought of as the "npm file". As the file extension would suggest, it must be in the **JavaScript Object Notation (JSON)** data format. If the JSON syntax is invalid, npm will display an error when reading this file. Using a `package.json` file in our project has many benefits. These include: making it easy to reinstall our dependencies by defining a dependencies field; letting us publish our module to npm by defining the `name` and `version` fields, and storing common scripts related to the package by defining the `scripts` object.

For a project using Grunt, the `dependencies` property will be the most useful feature of the `package.json` file. When we run the command: `npm install` (without a proceeding package name), npm will look for our `package.json`, parse it, then install each module listed in the `dependencies` property.

Before we review an example `package.json` file using the `dependencies` property it is important to understand how all npm packages are versioned. Tom Preston-Werner proposed the **Semantic Versioning** specification (**SemVer**) in late 2009, due to what he describes as "dependency hell" – a situation that arises within large systems built with many smaller systems. The SemVer website (http://gswg.io#semver) contains the following short summary:

> "Given a version number MAJOR.MINOR.PATCH, increment the:
>
> 1. MAJOR version when you make incompatible API changes,
>
> 2. MINOR version when you add functionality in a backwards-compatible manner, and
>
> 3. PATCH version when you make backwards-compatible bug fixes.
>
> Additional labels for pre-release and build metadata are available as extensions to the MAJOR.MINOR.PATCH format."

Although module publishers aren't required to strictly follow SemVer, npm does require them to ensure version numbers are in the correct format and incremented at each release.

The following is an exceptionally simple example of a `package.json` file:

```
//Code example 03-npm-install
{
  "dependencies": {
    "grunt": "0.4.2"
  }
}
```

In this case, when we execute: `npm install` alongside this `package.json` file, it is equivalent to executing: `npm install grunt@0.4.2`. The `@` symbol followed by the version tells npm to install that specific version of the `grunt` module. Grunt is a rare exception to rules above. Again, on to SemVer website:

> *"Major version zero (0.y.z) is for initial development. Anything may change at any time. The public API should not be considered stable."*

Since Grunt is currently at version 0.4.2 and also adheres to SemVer, the Grunt team considers Grunt to still be in development, as the API has not been frozen yet. Some disagree with this decision as Grunt is used so widely across the Web development industry; however, this is a relatively inconsequential detail. Since Grunt has no major version to make use of, the minor version is incremented for backward incompatible changes. Therefore, the changes made from version 0.3.x to 0.4.x of Grunt are incompatible. To prevent automatic upgrades of major and minor versions, we'll use tilde-prefixed versions. The tilde symbol (~) denotes any approximate version; this is a feature of npm, which can also been seen as an addition to SemVer to mitigate backward incompatible changes. The tilde prefix tells npm that it may only upgrade the given package for increments of the patch version. For example, if we first installed version 0.3.5 of the `grunt` module, while also specifying: `"grunt": "latest"` in our `package.json` file, subsequent npm installs would yield the latest version. As previously mentioned, a change from version 0.3.5 to 0.4.2 (latest), would introduce breaking changes to our build. However, if we instead specified the approximate version: `"grunt": "~0.3.5"`, subsequent npm installs would only upgrade us to a version matching 0.3.x, so currently, it would yield version 0.3.17.

For this reason, we should always specify the exact or approximate versions, we should never use `"latest"` or `"*"` (which means any version). To help us achieve best practice, a convenience option was added to npm for exactly this situation. When starting a project, and when we're installing a module for the first time, we can use the `--save` option, which in addition to installing the module will also automatically update our `package.json` file with the modules just installed and their latest approximate versions.

For example, if we started with an empty `package.json` file as follows:

```
{}
```

Then, if we executed: `npm install --save grunt grunt-contrib-uglify`, it would currently update our previously empty `package.json` file to the following code:

```
{
  "dependencies": {
    "grunt": "~0.4.2",
    "grunt-contrib-uglify": "~0.2.2"
  }
}
```

> As displayed in this example, when installing modules from npm, we can also include multiple module names at once `npm install module1 module2 module3`.

When we use `npm install`, npm will retrieve the given module and then its dependencies, and repeat this step until all dependencies have been retrieved. If we were to publish our module with the `grunt` module as a dependency, other modules, which depend on our module, would then be forced to download `grunt` too. Grunt, however, is a build tool; it builds and transforms our source into a final product. This final product is what should be published for public use. Therefore, in this case, the `grunt` module is a development-only dependency, and actually belongs in the `devDependencies` field of our `package.json` file. Luckily, there is also a `--save-dev` option, which will do exactly the same thing as the `--save` option, but instead of placing the dependencies listed in the `dependencies` field, it will use the `devDependencies` field.

As we add more and more fields to our `package.json` file, it can be tiresome setting it up again and we may be tempted to simply copy and paste the `package.json` file into a new project. It's good practice, however, to build our own `package.json` file for every project. This can be done easily with another npm feature, the `npm init` command. `npm init` is a setup "wizard" for creating `package.json` files. Once executed, npm will prompt us for each common field. This is a good habit to get into as, in most cases, the only similar field across all your projects will be the `author` field and there is an npm command for this too: `npm config set init.author.name 'Jaime Pillora'`. This will set the default author for all subsequent `npm init`. We especially should not copy and paste our `dependencies` field when starting a new project. The time when there is no code to break is the perfect time to upgrade to the latest version of each package.

Setting Up Grunt

In summary, when starting a new Grunt project, first we should create our `package.json` file with `npm init`, and then we should add our dependencies (Grunt as well as the Grunt plugins we're using) and also lock their current (and newest) version, for example, `npm install --save-dev grunt grunt-contrib-uglify`.

Once complete, we should have a `package.json` file that looks similar to the following one:

```
//Code example 04-package-json
{
  "name": "gswg-2-04-package-json",
  "version": "0.1.0",
  "repository": "https://github.com/jpillora/gswg-examples.git",
  "author": "Jaime Pillora <gswg@jpillora.com>",
  "devDependencies": {
    "grunt-contrib-uglify": "~0.2.2",
    "grunt": "~0.4.2"
  },
  "license": "MIT"
}
```

> We can confirm that we've created a valid `package.json` file by pasting its contents into this Package.json Validator tool found at http://gswg.io#package-json-validator.

Gruntfile.js

Just as the command `npm install` looks for the `package.json` file and fails without it, the `grunt` command will look for the `Gruntfile.js` file using a similar method as well. Once found, Grunt will invoke this file with the `grunt` global object. The `Gruntfile.js` file can be seen as our build initializer – it will define configuration and set up tasks. It will not, however, contain the directive to run the build. This happens automatically once the `Gruntfile.js` has finished executing. However, we can customize what is run, and we can provide extra options via the command line, as we will see in *Chapter 3, Using Grunt*.

On the getting started page on the Grunt website (http://gswg.io#grunt-getting-started), the Grunt team describes the following code as the `Gruntfile.js` file "wrapper":

```
module.exports = function(grunt) {
// Do grunt-related things in here
};
```

We could view this syntax as the magic "wrapping" that all `Gruntfile.js` files need in order to run; however, it is favorable to understand its purpose. If we recall our summary of CommonJS, we'll remember that the `module.exports` object is returned as the result of another module requiring it. Therefore, in this code, we're simply providing a function with a single parameter. Grunt will then call our function with the `grunt` object as the single argument. The `grunt` object is what we'll use to interact with Grunt. That is, it is Grunt's **Application Programming Interface (API)** – it contains the methods that have been exposed (or exported) for public use. The `grunt` object contains methods for updating and retrieving configuration (`grunt.config`), methods for loading and registering tasks (`grunt.task`), methods for reading and writing files (`grunt.file`), and much more. The `grunt` object also contains aliases to common functions, for example, `grunt.config.init` can be called via `grunt.initConfig` and `grunt.task.registerTask` can be called via `grunt.registerTask`.

Read more about the Grunt API at `http://gswg.io#grunt-api`.

> Since Grunt is open source, when we're unsure about a particular feature, we can always visit the repository and read the source code at `http://gswg.io#grunt-source-code`. Each feature set has its own file. For example, the `grunt.config` module and its methods can be found in the `lib/grunt/config.js` file.

The purpose of the "wrapper" function that we provide is to initialize our Grunt configuration for use within our tasks, and to load and group our tasks for use with the command line.

Now that we have a `package.json` file and installed our modules, we've just completed the prelude to `Code example 01-minify` at the beginning of this book. There, we'll find a simple `Gruntfile.js` file utilizing the `grunt-contrib-uglify` plugin and the expected output from executing this build. In the next section on configuring tasks, we'll cover more complex use cases.

Directory structure

Now that we've created our `package.json` and `Gruntfile.js` files and installed our packages, we should have the following directory structure:

```
//Code example 05-directory-structure
.
├── Gruntfile.js
├── package.json
└── node_modules
```

```
├── grunt
└── grunt-contrib-uglify
```

As an aside, if we're placing our project in a **Version Control System** (**VCS**), we'll need to remember to exclude the `node_modules` folder. For example, with Git we'd also include a `.gitignore` file containing a line `node_modules`.

Depending on the type of project, our source files may be structured differently, however, the common use case for Grunt is to transform our source files into our `build` (or `output`) files. So generally, we'll include all our source files in a folder called `src` and then create another folder `build` to house the result of this build. This clear separation is important because the `build` folder can then be seen as temporary: it may be replaced at any time with a new set of files. Therefore, it's important we do not get our `source` and `build` files mixed up.

If we were to add a test suite to our project, we'd also have the test files in addition to our `source` files. These test files exercise our `build` files to ensure they are functioning as expected. Finally, once we've added our project-related files, we should be left with a directory structure similar to the following one:

```
//Code example 05-directory-structure
.
├── Gruntfile.js
├── package.json
├── node_modules
│   ├── grunt
│   └── grunt-contrib-uglify
├── build
├── src
├── test
└── .gitignore
```

Also, by excluding the `build` folder from our VCS, we force all developers using this project to execute the build. This will highlight any machine-dependent build issues and ensure they are resolved early. Once in place, we have a trivial set-up guide to get started on our new project. Run `npm install` followed by `grunt`.

Configuring tasks

Grunt configuration can be thought of as single JavaScript object, though, instead of assigning values, we'll use functions provided by Grunt to get and set properties.

We briefly touched on Grunt configuration in *Chapter 1, Introducing Grunt*, displaying simple uses of the `grunt.initConfig`, `grunt.config.get` and `grunt.config.set` functions. The `grunt.initConfig` function (which as mentioned earlier, is aliased from `grunt.config.init`) accepts an object, which is then used as the starting point for our configuration, whereas the `grunt.config.get` and `grunt.config.set` functions are used to get and set individual properties. We can also use the shorter `grunt.config` function, which works like jQuery getters and setters. When called with one argument it aliases to `grunt.config.get`, and with two arguments, it aliases to `grunt.config.set`. Each line in the following example is functionally equivalent:

```
grunt.config.init({ foo: { bar: 7 }});
grunt.config.set('foo.bar', 7);
grunt.config('foo.bar', 7);
```

It's important to note that calls to `grunt.config.init` (or `grunt.initConfig`) will erase all prior configuration.

Grunt has a focus on declaratively defining a build. Since we use a build tool to improve our effectiveness, for our team and ourselves, it's important our build is manageable and accessible. If our build tool were simply a long shell (or batch) script of many steps, each process would be defined imperatively in sequence. Its length would make it difficult for others (and our future selves) to understand, forcing us to reverse engineer the steps. Whereas if our build were made up of declarative steps, we could read it like, "I'd like to compile these **CoffeeScript** files into this folder using these options". For example:

```
coffee: {
  compile: {
    files: {
      'build/app.js': 'src/scripts/**/*.coffee'
    },
    options: {
       bare: true
    }
  }
}
```

Therefore, we can view a Grunt configuration as a way to declaratively define how we wish to run imperative Grunt tasks. This is where Grunt shines and why it has become so popular – it helps to abstract the "how" and focuses on the "what".

Setting Up Grunt

The Grunt configuration methods may be used anywhere with access to the `grunt` object, however, in most cases we will only use our configuration within tasks and multitasks.

As described previously, Grunt tasks are just functions. For example, let's say we have a Grunt task to check for stray `console.log` statements in our `app.js` file. This `consoleCheck` task may look like:

```
//Code example 06-config-get-set
// tasks/console-check.js
module.exports = function(grunt) {

  grunt.registerTask('consoleCheck', function() {
    //load app.js
    var contents = grunt.file.read('./src/app.js');
    //search for console.log statements
    if(contents.indexOf('console.log(') >= 0)
      grunt.fail.warn('"console.log(" found in "app.js"');
  });

};
```

However, we may wish to reuse this task in another project. To assist with reusability, we'll generalize this task to be a string checking task by allowing us to define which file and what string to look for:

```
//Code example 06-config-get-set
// tasks/string-check.js
module.exports = function(grunt) {

  grunt.registerTask('stringCheck', function() {
    //fail if configuration is not provided
    grunt.config.requires('stringCheck.file');
    grunt.config.requires('stringCheck.string');

    //retrieve filename and load it
    var file = grunt.config('stringCheck.file');
    var contents = grunt.file.read(file);
    //retrieve string to search for
    var string = grunt.config('stringCheck.string');

    if(contents.indexOf(string >= 0))
      grunt.fail.warn('"' + string + '" found in "' + file + '"');
  });

};
```

First, in our new `stringCheck` task, we're using `grunt.config.requires` to ensure our configuration exists, next we're retrieving this configuration, and finally we'll search for the string and display the result. We can now configure this task to perform its original purpose by providing the following configuration:

```
//Code example 06-config-get-set
// Gruntfile.js
grunt.initConfig({
  stringCheck: {
    file: './src/app.js',
    string: 'console.log('
  }
});
```

When running this example with `console.log(` in our `app.js` file, we should see the following output:

```
$ grunt
Running "stringCheck" task
Warning: "console.log(" found in "./src/app.js"
Use --force to continue.

Aborted due to warnings.
```

On the last line of our output, we see that Grunt was aborted due to warnings. Since we used the `grunt.fail.warn` function in our task, we see the hint to use the `--force` flag to continue; however, if we were to use the `grunt.fail.fatal` function, we would not be able to ignore our new task until we remove the offending string. See the code examples to view the runnable version.

Also note this is a naïve approach to checking source code. For instance, this task would incorrectly fail when our string was commented out. To resolve this issue, we would need to use a JavaScript parser to extract the code's **Abstract Syntax Tree (AST)**, and then search this tree for syntax of our choosing.

Configuring multitasks

Continuing with our string checker task, we will most likely want to check more than one file. Instead of the file string, we may initially consider using a files array; however, what if we wanted to check for numerous strings in a single file? Should we also convert the `string` property into an array? And what if we only wanted to look for certain strings in certain files? Using arrays would not suffice.

Setting Up Grunt

Enter multitasks. Multitasks allow us to solve the hypothetical problems outlined previously using configuration targets. Targets provide us with the means to configure multiple runs of a single task. If we were to convert our string checker task into a multitask, its configuration might look like:

```
grunt.initConfig({
  stringCheck: {
    target1: {
      file: './src/app.js',
      string: 'console.log('
    },
    target2: {
      file: './src/util.js',
      string: 'eval('
    }
  }
});
```

We may recall similar configurations from *Chapter 1, Introducing Grunt*, code examples, which also use `target1` and `target2`. These generic names are used on purpose to reinforce the notion that target names may be arbitrarily set. We should therefore devise target names that improve the readability of our build. Many examples on the Internet display task names, such as `dist` (short for distribution), `build`, and `compile`. Although these might describe the target well, for a Grunt newcomer, it can be hard to discern which portions of the configuration must be static and which can be dynamic. For example, in the previous snippet of code, we could have used `app` and `util` instead of `target1` and `target2`. These logical names would improve the usability of our build by allowing us to use readable commands like:

```
$ grunt stringCheck:app
$ grunt stringCheck:util
```

In *Chapter 3, Using Grunt*, we'll learn more on running and creating our own multitasks.

Configuring options

Defining options to customize a task is quite common; hence, both tasks and multitasks have their function context set to the `Task` object, which has an `options` function available. When called, it looks for the task's configuration by name and then looks for the `options` object. For example:

```
grunt.initConfig({
  myTask: {
```

```
    options: {
      bar: 7
    },
    foo: 42
  }
});

grunt.registerTask('myTask', function() {
  this.options(); // { bar:7 }
});
```

This feature is most useful in multitasks as we are able to define a task-wide options object, which may be overridden by our target-specific options. For example:

```
grunt.initConfig({
  myMultiTask: {
    options: {
      foo: 42,
      bar: 7
    },
    target1: {
    },
    target2: {
      options: {
        bar: 8
      }
    }
  }
});
```

As `target1` does not have an `options` object defined, retrieving its options will yield: `{ foo:42, bar:7 }`. However, when we retrieve `target2` options, its bar option will override the task options and the resulting object will be: `{ foo:42, bar:8 }`. We will cover more on the `Task` object in *Chapter 3, Using Grunt*.

Configuring files

A vast majority of Grunt tasks will perform some kind of file operation. To cater for this, Grunt uses a predefined object structure along with file "globbing" (or wildcard file selection) to produce a succinct API for describing files. While running a multitask, its configuration will be checked for this file pattern and it will attempt to match the files it describes with what it can find at those locations. Once complete, it will place all matching files in the task's files array (`this.files` within the context of a task).

Next, we will cover the various ways that we can describe files for various use cases. Firstly, however, we'll discuss what it means to match a file. File matching within Grunt uses a module written by Isaac Schlueter: `node-glob`. File globbing comes from Unix in the 70s, when a simple language was invented to allow wildcard selection of files. For example, `*.txt` will match both `a.txt` and `b.txt`. Here is an extract from the Grunt documentation describing globbing options available in Grunt (http://gswg.io#grunt-globbing):

> "While this isn't a comprehensive tutorial on globbing patterns, know that in a filepath:
>
> `*` *matches any number of characters, but not* `/`
>
> `?` *matches a single character, but not* `/`
>
> `**` *matches any number of characters, including* `/`, *as long as it's the only thing in a path part*
>
> `{}` *allows for a comma-separated list of "or" expressions*
>
> `!` *at the beginning of a pattern will negate the match*
>
> *All most people need to know is that* `foo/*.js` *will match all files ending with* `.js` *in the* `foo/` *subdirectory, but* `foo/**/*.js` *will match all files ending with* `.js` *in the* `foo/` *subdirectory and all of its subdirectories."*

Next, we'll review portions of `Code example 07-config-files`. This example contains one task `showTargetFiles`, which displays the `files` array of each of its targets:

```
// Register a multitask (runs once per target)
grunt.registerMultiTask('showTargetFiles', function() {
  // Show the 'files' array
  this.files.forEach(function(file) {
    console.log ("source: " + file.src + " -> " +
             "destination: " + file.dest);
  });
});
```

Based on this task, we'll notice that each `file` in the `files` array contains `src` and `dest` properties. The `src` property in this case is the output from matching the input globs against the filesystem. Each of the following target examples contains `src` inputs and also the result of this task.

Single set of source files

This is the compact format; the target may describe one set source of files using the `src` property, along with an optional destination file using the `dest` property. Without a destination, this format is typically used for read-only tasks, like code analysis such as our string checker task:

```
target1: {
  src: ['src/a.js', 'src/b.js']
}
```

We could shorten the preceding example using the {} syntax described earlier, to denote a or b. We will also add a destination property:

```
target1: {
  src: 'src/{a,b}.js',
  dest: 'dest/ab.js'
}
```

Notice that we have left out the array in this second example as it is not required since we're specifying only one glob string. If we wanted to define multiple sets of source files, we would need to use the `files` property.

Multiple sets of source files

To describe multiple source sets with single destination, we can use the "Files array format". For example, this format could be useful when describing multiple file concatenations:

```
target1: {
  files: [
    { src: 'src/{a,b,c}.js', dest: 'dest/abc.js' },
    { src: 'src/{x,y,z}.js', dest: 'dest/xyz.js' }
  ]
}
```

We can get an equivalent result with the more compressed: "Files object format", where the `files` property is now an object instead of an array, with each key being the destination and each value being the source, as follows:

```
target1: {
  files: {
    'dest/abc.js': 'src/{a,b,c}.js',
    'dest/xyz.js': 'src/{x,y,z}.js'
  }
}
```

Moreover, when we specify a set of files using an object with `src` and `dest`, we have the choice to use some additional options; one of these options will allow us to map directories as opposed to files.

Mapping a source directory to destination directory

Often we would like to convert a set of source files into the same set of destination files. In this case, we're essentially choosing a source directory and a destination directory. This is useful when compiling CoffeeScript (or any other source-to-source compilation) and we'd like to maintain the directory structure, whilst still running each individual file via the transform of our choosing. This is done using the expand option. For instance, if we wanted to compress all of our `.js` source files into a result set of the `.min.js` files, we could manually map each file from one directory to another:

```
target1: {
  files: [
    {src: 'lib/a.js', dest: 'build/a.min.js'},
    {src: 'lib/b.js', dest: 'build/b.min.js'},
    {src: 'lib/subdir/c.js', dest: 'build/subdir/c.min.js'},
    {src: 'lib/subdir/d.js', dest: 'build/subdir/d.min.js'},
  ],
}
```

However, with each file addition, we will need to add another line of configuration. With the `expand` option, a destination for each of matched source files will be automatically generated based on the source file's path and additional options. Here, `target2` is equivalent to `target1`, however as we add new source files, they will automatically be matched by our `'**/*.js'` glob string and mapped to the appropriate destination file:

```
target2: {
  files: [
    {
      expand: true,
      cwd: 'lib/',
      src: '**/*.js',
      dest: 'build/',
      ext: '.min.js'
    },
  ],
}
```

Here are the additional options available at http://gswg.io#configuring-tasks for use inside any file object:

"expand *Set to* true *to enable the following options:*

cwd *All* src *matches are relative to (but don't include) this path.*

src *Pattern(s) to match, relative to the* cwd.

dest *Destination path prefix.*

ext *Replace any existing extension with this value in generated* dest *paths.*

flatten *Remove all path parts from generated* dest *paths.*

rename *This function is called for each matched* src *file, (after extension renaming and flattening). The* dest *and matched* src *path are passed in, and this function must return a new* dest *value. If the same* dest *is returned more than once, each* src *which used it will be added to an array of sources for it."*

Refer to Code example 07-config-files for demonstrations of each file configuration method.

Templates

In the preceding configuration section, we covered the use of grunt.config. Here, we cover one of the reasons why we use a special "getter" and "setter" API to modify a simple object. When we set values in our configuration with grunt.config.set or grunt.initConfig, we can use the Grunt template system to reuse other portions of our configuration. For example, if we defined some properties:

```
//Code Example 08-templates
grunt.initConfig({
  foo: 'c',
  bar: 'b<%= foo %>d',
  bazz: 'a<%= bar %>e'
});
```

Then, if we run the task:

```
//Code Example 08-templates
grunt.registerTask('default', function() {
    grunt.log.writeln( grunt.config.get('bazz') );
});
```

We should see:

```
$ grunt
Running "default" task
abcde
```

When we use `grunt.config.get("...")`, internally Grunt is using the `grunt.template.process` function to resolve each template recursively (that is, we can have templates inside other templates). Grunt templates are most useful when we wish to perform many tasks on a single set of files. We can define this set once and then use Grunt templates to re-use it multiple times. For example, with the following configuration:

```
//Code example 09-templates-array
grunt.initConfig({
  foo: ['a.js','b.js','c.js','d.js'],
  bazz: '<%= foo %>'
});
```

Our preceding task returns:

```
Running "default" task
[ 'a.js', 'b.js', 'c.js', 'd.js' ]
```

When using the `grunt.config.get` function to retrieve the `bazz` property, it does not return a string, since `bazz` only contains the template reference to `foo`. Instead, it is replaced by the `foo` array.

Summary

At this point, we have Node.js along with npm installed on our machine. We have the npm module `grunt-cli` installed globally, providing us with the `grunt` executable. We understand the basic premise of how modules work in Node.js and we know how to find and install modules from npm. Lastly, we understand the purpose of the `package.json` file and the `Gruntfile.js` file. In the next chapter, we will learn how to create our own tasks using Grunt.

3
Using Grunt

Now that we've installed and configured Grunt, we're ready to use it. In this chapter, we'll review creating our own tasks and cover the finer points omitted in previous chapters. We shall also cover the various methods of executing tasks over and above simply running Grunt on the command-line. Finally, we will cover how to choose the most appropriate tasks for the job and exactly how to integrate them into our Grunt build.

Creating your own tasks

In this section, we shall explore the creation of Grunt tasks in more detail, specifically normal tasks and multitasks, and asynchronous tasks.

Tasks

As exemplified previously, creating tasks is extremely simple. We provide a name and a function to grunt.registerTask and we're ready to execute. Tasks (as opposed to multitasks) are best suited to build processes that will only be performed once in a given build. A real world example of such a process might be to update a deployment log file, which we could run whenever we deploy, providing a simple history of deployments for future reference. This task might look like:

```
//Code example 01-deploy-log-task
var fs = require('fs');
module.exports = function(grunt) {
  grunt.registerTask('log-deploy', function() {
    var message = 'Deployment on ' + new Date();
    fs.appendFileSync('deploy.log', message + '\n');
    grunt.log.writeln('Appended "' + message + '"');
  });
};
```

Using Grunt

> See the Node.js API documentation for more information on each built-in module: `http://gswg.io#node-api`.

On the first line, we are requiring (or importing) the built-in Node.js file system module: `fs`. Then, inside our `log-deploy` task, we'll use the `fs.appendFileSync` method which will append arbitrary text to a given file (first creating the file, if it doesn't exist). When we run this task, it should create a `deploy.log` file and display:

```
$ grunt log-deploy
Running "log-deploy" task
Appended "Deployment on Wed Aug 28 2013 20:43:54 GMT+1000 (EST)"

Done, without errors.
```

The task object

We can access the properties of the task currently running via the `grunt.current.task` object. When tasks are executed, the current task object is used as the function context, where it may also be accessed via the JavaScript `this` operator.

The task object has the following properties:

- `name` – a string set to the task name (the first parameter provided to `grunt.registerTask`).
- `async` – a function which notifies Grunt that this task is asynchronous and returns a callback. There is more on this in the *Asynchronous tasks* section.
- `requires` – a function which accepts an array of task names (strings), then ensures that they have previously run. So, if we had a `deploy` task we might use `this.requires(["compile"])`, which will ensure we have compiled our code before we deploy it.
- `requiresConfig` – an alias to the `grunt.config.requires` function, briefly touched on in *Chapter 2, Setting Up Grunt*. This function causes the current task to fail if a given path configuration property does not exist.
- `nameArgs` – a string set as the task name including arguments used when running the task.
- `args` – an array of all arguments used to run the task.
- `flags` – an object which uses each of the `args` as its keys and `true` as the value. This allows us to use the arguments as a series of switches. So, if we ran the task `foo` with `grunt foo:one:two`, then `this.flags.two` would be `true` but `this.flags.three` would be `undefined` (which is falsy).

- `errorCount` – a number representing the number of calls to `grunt.log.error`.
- `options` – a function used to retrieve the task's configuration options which is functionally equivalent to `grunt.config.get([this.name, "options"])`. However, in the next section on multitasks, the `options` function becomes more useful.

The following is a simple example demonstrating the use of the task object:

```
//Code example 02-task-object
module.exports = function(grunt) {

  grunt.registerTask('foo', function() {
    console.log('My task "%s" has arguments %j',
                this.name, this.args);
  });

};
```

Now, if we run this task with `grunt foo:bar:bazz` we should see:

```
$ grunt foo:bar:bazz
Running "foo:bar:bazz" (foo) task
My task "foo" has arguments ["bar","bazz"]

Done, without errors.
```

For more information on the task object, refer to http://gswg.io#grunt-task-object, and for more information on the `this` operator in JavaScript, refer to http://gswg.io#this-operator.

Task aliasing

Instead of providing a function to `grunt.registerTask`, we can also provide an array of strings; this will create a new task that will sequentially run each of the tasks listed in the array, essentially allowing us to give a name to a set of other tasks. For example, we could create three tasks: `build`, `test`, and `upload`, then alias them as a new task `upload` by using the following code:

```
//Code example 03-task-aliasing
module.exports = function(grunt) {

  grunt.registerTask('build', function() {
    console.log('building...');
  });
```

[57]

```
  grunt.registerTask('test', function() {
    console.log('testing...');
  });

  grunt.registerTask('upload', function() {
    console.log('uploading...');
  });

  grunt.registerTask('deploy', ['build', 'test', 'upload']);
};
```

So, when we run `grunt deploy`, it will perform all three tasks in sequence:

```
$ grunt deploy
Running "build" task
building...

Running "test" task
testing...

Running "upload" task
uploading...

Done, without errors.
```

Now, let's assume that our build process was more complex. We could further divide up each of these three tasks into smaller subtasks. For instance, our fictitious `build` task above could also be an alias made up of build-related tasks, such as `compile-coffee-script`, `compile-tests`, `copy-html`, and so on. In the next section, we'll see that multitasks fit the mold of most build processes, and therefore, when it comes time to name (or alias) a set of tasks, we'll most likely be referencing multitasks and their targets.

Multitasks

As with many build tools, the majority of Grunt tasks perform static checks or transforms on groups of files. This was the impetus for the introduction of multitasks. As we have seen in previous chapters, multitasks are like tasks, however, they accept multiple configurations. Grunt will use each property (except `options`) of a multi task's configuration as an individual configuration, called a target. This allows us to define a single task which is capable of being run many times, each time performing different actions based on each configuration. For example, let's review how we would implement a `copy` multitask, which copies files based on a set of one-to-one (source to destination) mappings:

```
//Code example 04-copy-multi-task
grunt.registerMultiTask('copy', function() {

  this.files.forEach(function(file) {
    grunt.file.copy(file.src, file.dest);
  });

  grunt.log.writeln('Copied ' + this.files.length + ' files');
});
```

This task iterates through the `this.files` array copying each `file` object's source (`src`) to its destination (`dest`). In order to run this task, we must define at least one target. So, let's initialize our `copy` task configuration with two targets, each with two simple file mappings:

```
//Code example 04-copy-multi-task
grunt.initConfig({
  copy: {
    target1: {
      files: {
        'dest/file1.txt': 'src/file1.txt',
        'dest/file2.txt': 'src/file2.txt'
      }
    },
    target2: {
      files: {
        'dest/file3.txt': 'src/file3.txt',
        'dest/file4.txt': 'src/file4.txt'
      }
    }
  }
});
```

We can now run `target2` of the `copy` task using the command `grunt copy:target2`, which should result in:

```
$ grunt copy:target2
Running "copy:target2" (copy) task
Copied 2 files

Done, without errors.
```

Using Grunt

Furthermore, if we omit the target name and simply use the command, `grunt copy`, then Grunt will run all targets of the `copy` task:

```
$ grunt copy
Running "copy:target1" (copy) task
Copied 2 files

Running "copy:target2" (copy) task
Copied 2 files

Done, without errors.
```

Remember, the `this.files` array is filled with file objects using the methods described in the *Configuring Files* section in *Chapter 2, Setting Up Grunt*. This brings us to the next section on the multitask object.

The multitask object

As with tasks, we can access task properties of the currently running multitask via the `grunt.current.task` property. Similarly, the multitask object is set as the function context (the `this` operator) when the task is invoked. In addition to all of properties of the `task` object, the multitask object contains the following:

- `target` – a string set to the target name (the property name used inside our Grunt configuration).
- `files` – an array of file objects. Each object will have an `src` property and an optional `dest` property. This array is useful when we have described sets of files for use in a transform, where there are source (or input) files and optional destination (or output) files.
- `filesSrc` – an array of strings representing only the `src` property of each file object from the above `files` array. This array is useful for when we have described sets of source files and we have no use for destination files. For instance, plugins that perform static analysis, like JSHint, would only require source files.
- `data` – which is the target object itself. It is best used as a fallback if the `files` array and the `options` function don't provide the functionality necessary. In most cases, the use of this property is not required.

Although the `options` function also exists on the task object, the `options` function on the multitask object performs an extra step:

- `options` – a function used to retrieve the combination of the task's and target's configuration options. This is functionally equivalent to merging the results of `grunt.config.get([this.name, "options"])` and `grunt.config.get([this.name, this.target, "options"])`. This is useful because the user of the task can set task-wide defaults and then, within each target, they can override these defaults with a set of target-specific options.

For more information on the multitask object, see `http://gswg.io#grunt-task-object`.

Asynchronous tasks

Synchronous tasks are considered complete as soon as the task function returns. However, in some cases we may need to utilize libraries with asynchronous APIs. These APIs will have functions that provide their results via callbacks instead of the return statement. If we were to use an asynchronous API in a synchronous task, this would cause Grunt report success (no errors detected) and incorrectly continue onto the next task in the list.

As described previously, both the task object and the multitask object contain an `async` function, which notifies Grunt that the current task is asynchronous and also returns a `done` function. This `done` function is used to manually control the result of our task. For example, we could create a task that retrieves a file using HTTP and stores the contents on disk:

```
//Code example 05-async-webget
var request = require('request');
var url = 'https://raw.github.com/jpillora/'+
          'gswg-examples/master/README.md';

module.exports = function(grunt) {
  grunt.registerTask('webget', function() {
    var done = this.async();
    request(url, function(err, response, contents) {
      if(err) {
        done(err);
      } else if(response.statusCode !== 200) {
        done(new Error('Not OK'));
      } else {
        grunt.file.write('FILE.md', contents);
        grunt.log.ok('FILE.md successfully created');
        done();
```

```
      }
    });
  });
};
```

At the top of our example `Gruntfile.js`, we are requiring the popular module for performing HTTP requests: `request`. Since `request` performs an asynchronous HTTP request, we'll use the task object's `async` function (`this.async()`) to both place this task in asynchronous mode, and then retrieve the `done` function. Subsequently, we can signal failure to Grunt by passing an `Error` object or `false` to the `done` function. Anything else will signal success.

In this example, once we've received the response we shall first check that there were no errors with sending the request. If there are errors, we'll pass the `err` object straight to `done`. Next, we'll check if we received `response` successfully by confirming that the HTTP `statusCode` is `200`. If it is not, we will pass our own custom error `"Not OK"` to `done`. Once both error checks have passed, we can finally write the response's `contents` to disk and then call `done()`, informing Grunt that this asynchronous task has completed successfully. So, when we run this task, we should see:

```
$ grunt webget
Running "webget" task
>> FILE.md successfully created

Done, without errors.
```

Running tasks

Up until this point, we have learnt how to configure and create tasks. Now it is time to run them!

Command-line

Some Node.js command-line tools, such as `express`, may also be used as a module, whereas Grunt may only be used via the command-line. Once we've globally installed the `grunt-cli` module, our system will have access to the `grunt` executable.

To run our newly loaded or created tasks, we need to provide Grunt with a list of task names as space-separated command-line arguments. This will result in Grunt executing each specified task in sequence; which means we can easily dictate the order of task execution. We could run `foo` then `bar` with:

```
$ grunt foo bar
```

Or, we run `bar` then `foo` with:

```
$ grunt bar foo
```

There is a special case, however, when we execute `grunt` on its own. Grunt interprets this as `grunt default` and subsequently will attempt to run the `default` task. Therefore, by registering a `default` task, we can make it easy to run our most common task. Similar to our previous example in the *Task aliasing* section, we could alias our `build` and `test` tasks as the `default` task with the following `Gruntfile.js` file:

```
//Code example 06-default-tasks
module.exports = function(grunt) {

  grunt.registerTask('build', function() {
    console.log('building...');
  });

  grunt.registerTask('test', function() {
    console.log('testing...');
  });

  grunt.registerTask('default', ['build', 'test']);
};
```

Now, we can simply run `grunt`, which should result in:

```
$ grunt
Running "build" task
building...

Running "test" task
testing...

Done, without errors.
```

We can run multitasks in a similar fashion; however, when we specify a multitask, Grunt will execute all of its targets. If we wanted to run a particular target then we can append it to the task name. So, if we wanted to run the `foo` task's `target1` target, then we would execute `grunt foo:target1`. For example, let's convert our `build` and `test` tasks in the previous example to multitasks and test this out:

```
//Code example 07-default-multi-tasks
module.exports = function(grunt) {
```

Using Grunt

```
grunt.initConfig({
  build: {
    main: {},
    extra: {}
  },
  test: {
    main: {},
    extra: {}
  }
});
grunt.registerMultiTask('build', function() {
  console.log('building target ' + this.target + '...');
});
grunt.registerMultiTask('test', function() {
  console.log('testing target ' + this.target + '...');
});
grunt.registerTask('default', ['build:main', 'test:main']);
};
```

We can explicitly run the build task's main target and then the test task's main target with:

```
$ grunt build:main test:main
Running "build:main" (build) task
building target main...

Running "test:main" (test) task
testing target main...

Done, without errors.
```

However, extending from the previous example, we could also add these targets in our default task alias. As you can see in the previous code, we have placed targets inside our array of task names, and therefore, when we run grunt we should see the same output:

```
$ grunt
Running "build:main" (build) task
building target main...

Running "test:main" (test) task
testing target main...

Done, without errors.
```

Task arguments

Additionally, when we specify a *task* we may also include an optional, colon-separated, list of arguments. For example, the following `Gruntfile.js` defines a `foo` task, which prints its first and second parameters:

```
//Code example 08-task-args
module.exports = function(grunt) {

  grunt.registerTask('foo', function(p1, p2) {
    console.log('first parameter is: ' + p1);
    console.log('second parameter is: ' + p2);
  });

};
```

Now, we can run the `foo` task with the arguments `bar` and `bazz` using:

```
$ grunt foo:bar:bazz
Running "foo:bar:bazz" (foo) task
first parameter is: bar
second parameter is: bazz

Done, without errors.
```

However, when we wish to run a multitask, before we can specify arguments we must first specify the target. Let's convert the previous example's `foo` task into a multitask:

```
//Code Example 09-multi-task-args
module.exports = function(grunt) {

  grunt.initConfig({
    foo: {
      ping: {},
      pong: {}
    }
  });

  grunt.registerMultiTask('foo', function(p1, p2) {
    console.log('target is: ' + this.target);
    console.log('first parameter is: ' + p1);
    console.log('second parameter is: ' + p2);
  });

};
```

Using Grunt

Similarly, but with the inclusion of `ping` as the target:

```
$ grunt foo:ping:bar:bazz
Running "foo:ping:bar:bazz" (foo) task
target is: ping
first parameter is: bar
second parameter is: bazz

Done, without errors.
```

With these examples in mind, we can see that we could create aliases which use tasks, multitasks, targets, and arguments all together, resulting in an extremely flexible build.

> Terminology Tip—When invoking a function, we provide it with arguments. When inside a function, we use its parameters. We can remember this with *arguments outside, parameters inside*.

Runtime options

Not to be confused with configuration options, runtime options must be specified on the command-line in addition to our list of tasks. Runtime options are used to create Grunt-wide settings for a single execution of Grunt. Runtime options must be prefixed with at least one dash, "-", otherwise they will be seen as task name. Runtime options are best used when one or many tasks have a configuration setting that we wish to modify only some of the time. For instance, when we execute Grunt we can enable our `optimize` option to direct each task specified to run in an optimized mode. This could remove debug statements, compress output, and so on. Once we've specified a runtime option on the command-line, we can retrieve its value using the `grunt.option` function.

For example, let's say we have the following `Gruntfile.js`:

```
//Code example 10-runtime-opts
module.exports = function(grunt) {
  console.log('bar is: ' + grunt.option('bar'));
  grunt.registerTask('foo', function() {
    //nothing here...
  });
};
```

Now, if we run this empty `foo` task with no options, we'll see:

```
$ grunt foo
bar is: undefined
Running "foo" task

Done, without errors.
```

Then, if we run this task again with the `bar` option set:

```
$ grunt foo --bar
bar is: true
Running "foo" task

Done, without errors.
```

If we like, we can give the `bar` option a specific value using the `=value` suffix:

```
$ grunt foo --bar=42
bar is: 42
Running "foo" task

Done, without errors.
```

In this case we are using the `grunt.option` function outside of the task. This is important since it means we can use our runtime options to assist with the configuration of our tasks. Note the `console.log` output occurs before the `"Running "foo" task"` output; this is because Grunt executes our `Gruntfile.js` in order to initialize our tasks and configuration, and *only* then the tasks specified on the command line are run in sequence.

For details on the Grunt Runtime Options API, refer to http://gswg.io#grunt-options. In *Chapter 4*, *Grunt in Action*, in the *Step 5 – tasks and options* section, we will review a technique to achieve environment specific builds through the use of runtime options.

Task help

When we are provided with an existing project for which there is no explicit documentation regarding the Grunt build, we can start off by listing the available tasks using the `grunt --help` command. When we use `grunt.registerTask` or `grunt.registerMultiTask`, we may optionally include a description. Let's review an example of this:

```
//Code example 11-task-help
module.exports = function(grunt) {
```

Using Grunt

```
      grunt.registerTask('analyze',
        'Analyzes the source',
        function() {
          console.log('analyzing...');
        }
      );

      grunt.registerMultiTask('compile',
        'Compiles the source',
        function() {
          console.log('compiling...');
        }
      );

      grunt.registerTask('all',
        'Analyzes and compiles the source',
        ['analyze','compile']
      );

   };
```

Now, if we run `grunt --help`, we should see the following excerpt within the output:

```
$ grunt --help
Grunt: The JavaScript Task Runner (v0.4.2)
Usage
 grunt [options] [task [task ...]]
...
Available tasks
       analyze  Analyzes the source
       compile  Compiles the source *
           all  Analyzes and compiles the source
...
```

The Grunt static help text has been omitted, leaving only the dynamic text. Here, we can see that Grunt has listed each of our tasks, along with its description, and multitasks are suffixed with a star `*`. This is useful because it might not be obvious to those new to this build that the `all` task runs both the `analyze` task and the `compile` task.

Programmatically

Although it is possible to execute Grunt from another program, it is intended to be used as a command-line utility, and therefore its API is only to be used with the `grunt` executable. We can, however, programmatically run tasks *within* other tasks, allowing us to conditionally run a series of tasks.

The following example is very similar to `Code example 04-linting` from *Chapter 1, Introducing Grunt*. This time, however, instead of defining our JSHint rules inside our `Gruntfile.js`, we are defining them in a portable `.jshintrc` file. This is favorable to some as it provides the ability to use a company-wide JavaScript coding style:

```
//Code example 12-conditional-lint
module.exports = function(grunt) {

  // Load the plugin that provides the "jshint" task.
  grunt.loadNpmTasks('grunt-contrib-jshint');
  // Project configuration.
  grunt.initConfig({
    jshint: {
      options: {
        jshintrc:'.jshintrc'
      },
      target1: 'src/**/*.js'
    }
  });
};
```

With this configuration, however, the `jshint` task will fail if the `.jshintrc` file is missing:

```
$ grunt jshint
Running "jshint:target1" (jshint) task
ERROR: Can't find config file: .jshintrc
```

Therefore, if we wanted to make our `jshint` task run only when we provide a `.jshintrc` file, then we could make another task that controls the execution of the `jshint` task:

```
// A new task to make "jshint" optional
grunt.registerTask('check', function() {
  if(grunt.file.exists('.jshintrc')) {
    grunt.task.run('jshint');
  }
});
```

Using Grunt

In our new `check` task, we shall first verify that the `.jshintrc` exists, and then we'll *programmatically* run the `jshint` task using the `grunt.task.run` function. Now, when we run the `check` task without a `.jshintrc` file, Grunt should do nothing and report success:

```
$ grunt check
Running "check" task


Done, without errors.
```

Though, when we include our `.jshintrc` file along side our `Gruntfile.js` and rerun our `check` task, we should see the following:

```
$ grunt check
Running "check" task


Running "jshint:target1" (jshint) task
>> 1 file lint free.


Done, without errors.
```

For an example of a `.jshintrc` file, please refer to http://gswg.io#jshintrc-example. For a summary of JavaScript Linting, please return to the *Static Analysis or Linting* section of *Chapter 1, Introducing Grunt*.

Automatically

One of the most popular Grunt plugins is `grunt-contrib-watch` (http://gswg.io#grunt-contrib-watch) as it allows us to place Grunt in the background and have it automatically run our tasks as they're needed. Written by *Kyle Robinson Young*, the `watch` task instructs Grunt to watch a particular set of files for changes and execute a particular task or set of tasks in response. In the following example, we'll watch our source files, and then run our JavaScript concatenation task `concat` whenever any of these files are changed:

```
//Code example 13-watch
module.exports = function(grunt) {

   // Load the plugins that provide the "concat" and "watch" tasks.
   grunt.loadNpmTasks('grunt-contrib-concat');
   grunt.loadNpmTasks('grunt-contrib-watch');

   // Project configuration.
```

```
    grunt.initConfig({
      srcFiles: ["src/a.js", "src/b.js", "src/c.js"],
      concat: {
        target1: {
          files: {
            "build/abc.js": "<%= srcFiles %>"
          }
        }
      },
      watch: {
        target1: {
          files: "<%= srcFiles %>",
          tasks: ["concat"]
        }
      }
    });

    // Define the default task
    grunt.registerTask('default', ['concat', 'watch']);
};
```

At the top of our `Gruntfile.js` file, we'll load both the plugins that provide the `concat` and `watch` tasks. We will then configure them using a shared `srcFiles` property. This means we can modify our source files once, and all tasks using this set of files will stay current. This helps to keep our build DRY (http://gswg.io#dry) by creating a single source of truth. All targets of the `watch` task (only `target1` in this case) require a `tasks` property that should specify a list of tasks to run when one of the target's `files` are changed. Finally, we'll provide a default task that runs `concat` followed by `watch`. Running `grunt` at this point should produce:

```
grunt
Running "concat:target1" (concat) task
File "build/abc.js" created.

Running "watch" task
Waiting...
```

At this point, our watch task is running and is `Waiting...` for one of our `files` to change; so if we modify and save `src/b.js`, we should see the following appended to our output:

```
OK
>> File "src/b.js" changed.

Running "concat:target1" (concat) task
```

```
File "build/abc.js" created.

Done, without errors.
Completed in 0.648s at Tue Sep 17 2013 21:57:52 GMT+1000 (EST)
Waiting...
```

Our `concat` task was run, and our `watch` task is `Waiting...` again, ready for more changes. Since we are watching our source files, we can now minimize our terminal window and continue with our development workflow, knowing that Grunt is running in the background, taking care of the "grunt" work for us.

Using third-party tasks

Although creating our own tasks is relatively straightforward, a vast number of plugins have already been implemented, providing tasks for many common use cases. Therefore, we should make sure we've thoroughly searched before we reinvent the wheel.

Searching for tasks

We've covered searching for modules in *Chapter 2, Setting Up Grunt*, in the section on *npm*, where we covered basic npm commands, including `npm search`. However, for those more comfortable with a web search, we can also use the Grunt website's plugin page (http://gswg.io#grunt-plugins). Once an hour, the Grunt team will execute `npm search gruntplugin` and store the results. When you visit the plugin page, this cached list will be retrieved and can be filtered by entering a query into the text input. Keep in mind, however, that even if a plugin was called `grunt-foo`, it would only be contained in this page if it were *also* tagged with `gruntplugin` (which some may forget to do). So when searching for preexisting plugins, we start with Grunt's plugin page, then move onto `npm search`, and finally we should resort to Google. Once we've found a set of candidate tasks, we will then need to decide which to use.

Official versus user tasks

The Grunt team has come up with a naming convention for all plugins that they officially support. Such plugins are prefixed with `grunt-contrib-`, whereas plugins created by the rest of the community are simply prefixed with `grunt-`. This allows us to easily discern between official Grunt plugins and user Grunt plugins.

Task popularity

The next step in our search for the appropriate plugin is to look at npm download statistics. These statistics can be found on the package page of all modules in the npm repository. For example, to view the download statistics for the Grunt plugin `grunt-contrib-uglify`, we can visit http://gswg.io#npm-package:grunt-contrib-uglify, and we should see:

> **grunt-contrib-uglify**
>
> Minify files with UglifyJS.
>
> $ npm install grunt-contrib-uglify
>
>   5 879   downloads in the last day
> 37 832   downloads in the last week
> 133 299   downloads in the last month

Here, we can see that this Grunt plugin was downloaded **133,299** times in the last month. This download count can be viewed as an implicit vote from each of the plugin's users.

Task features

A plugin's download count, however, doesn't necessarily mean it will have all of the features we need. For example, the `grunt-s3` plugin (http://gswg.io#npm-package:grunt-s3) is the most popular Amazon S3 Grunt plugin:

> **grunt-s3**
>
> A grunt task to automate moving files to/from Amazon S3.
>
> $ npm install grunt-s3
>
>   467   downloads in the last day
> 1 685   downloads in the last week
> 5 287   downloads in the last month

However, at the time this book was published, the Amazon S3 plugin was lacking a local cache (this results in higher bandwidth usage, which is suboptimal on a slow connection). Also, it was using the knox npm module to interface with S3, instead of the newly released, and officially supported, Amazon Node.js SDK aws-sdk. To remedy this, I wrote the grunt-aws plugin (http://gswg.io#npm-package:grunt-aws). Currently, grunt-aws is not as popular as grunt-s3, however, it has the features I require:

```
grunt-aws

A Grunt interface into the Amazon Node.JS SDK

$ npm install grunt-aws

 13  downloads in the last day
 87  downloads in the last week
436  downloads in the last month
```

Therefore, the download count is useful, though we should also view the plugin's documentation to ensure it supports the features we seek.

Task stars

As well as finding documentation on the task's GitHub repository, we will also find the task's star count. In recent years, GitHub has become the home for the majority of open source projects. Currently, 98 percent of all Grunt plugins have their source code on GitHub. All GitHub repositories have a list of stargazers, which are people who have starred that repository (or marked it as a favorite). This counter is displayed on each repository alongside the **Star** button, and this star count may be viewed as explicit votes, which vouch for the project's usefulness.

Summary

In summary, we should now be equipped with the knowledge to create our own tasks and multitasks using the full extent of features available to us. We should also be able to execute tasks in a wide variety of ways, and understand the situations in which to use runtime options, arguments, and when to simply use configuration. In the next chapter, we shall step through a complete example of building a Web Application from scratch using both Grunt, and the lessons we've learnt in these first three chapters.

4
Grunt in Action

It is now time to put our newfound knowledge into action. Grunt can be used in a wide variety of ways; however, the most common use case is a static website. Static websites are growing in popularity, as the web development industry requires ever-increasing levels of scalability. Although using a **Content Management System (CMS)** is a common method of managing a website, it is not the most efficient method of serving a website. This is because the majority of CMSs, such as **WordPress,** require PHP and an accompanying database. Static files on the other hand, can be hosted very cheaply on a cloud service such as Amazon's S3. Even if our website requires a server component to provide authentication, we may, for example, reduce the load on the server by moving as much logic as possible into the frontend. This provides us with a greater ability to scale, while reducing costs at the same time. We can take this idea of scalability even further with the concept of single-page applications. Traditionally, each page we view requires the server to answer requests for the same set of assets over and over, while also providing dynamic HTML for that given page. In a single-page application, as the name suggests, the website is made up of only one page. This single page intelligently responds to user interaction, hence its description as an application instead of a website. In this chapter, we start from scratch and carefully go through the process of using Grunt to create the build for an optimized single-page application.

Creating the build

Let's look at the various steps involved in using Grunt to create the build for a single-page application.

Step 1 – initial directory setup

We begin our project by creating a root directory, `project`. Within this directory, we create an `src` directory to house our source files. Then, we initialize the project's `package.json` file, install the local `grunt` module, and finally, create an empty `Gruntfile.js` file. We can do this on the command line with:

```
$ mkdir project
$ cd project/
$ mkdir src
$ npm init
$ npm install --save-dev grunt
$ echo "module.exports = function(grunt) {};" > Gruntfile.js
```

As we might expect, the `echo` command echoes the provided string back to the command line (which is known as standard out or "stdout"). The arrow (>), however, redirects standard out to a file. So, this last line is just a short way of creating and initializing a file. It is not necessary to create these files and directories on the command line, as long as we end up with the following directory structure:

```
//Code example 01-project
project/
├── Gruntfile.js
├── node_modules
│   └── grunt
├── package.json
└── src
```

At this point, we can now execute `grunt`, since we have no tasks; however, we should see the following command:

```
$ grunt
Warning: Task "default" not found. Use --force to continue.

Aborted due to warnings.
```

Step 2 – initial configuration

With many websites, including single-page applications, we can end up with an increasing amount of JavaScript, CSS, and HTML as they grow in complexity. We can improve code manageability by simply concatenating any number of individual files spread out across an organized set of folders. As well as splitting up our code into many files, we can also improve the code itself.

This is achieved through use of transcompile languages. In this step, we are using CoffeeScript, Stylus, and Jade, as each provides a minimalist syntax for its corresponding language. This minimalism improves readability by making our code cleaner and more succinct. For instance, a halving of the code required to produce the same result is often achieved. In addition to the cleaner syntax, there are added language features that can further increase productivity. For more information and examples of each, visit the following links:

- CoffeeScript (http://gswg.io#coffeescript)
- Stylus (http://gswg.io#stylus)
- Jade (http://gswg.io#jade)

However, we should keep in mind that there are alternatives to these three transcompile languages. We can easily swap out CoffeeScript for TypeScript or Dart, swap out Stylus for Sass or LESS, and swap out Jade for Haml or EJS. This replacement is easy because each of these defines a source code transformation, and since transcompiling Grunt plugins are mostly similar, our configuration should also look similar, regardless of which language we choose.

The programs that perform transcompilation are known as preprocessors. Therefore, Grunt plugins that perform transcompilation may be seen as thin wrappers around a given preprocessor. Now, we will install a Grunt plugin for each of our chosen languages and their corresponding preprocessors:

```
$ npm install --save-dev grunt-contrib-coffee grunt-contrib-jade grunt-contrib-stylus
```

> Both Stylus and Sass are very similar, however, Stylus is my CSS preprocessor of choice because the Stylus preprocessor is written in JavaScript, so it runs in Node.js; whereas the Sass preprocessor (http://gswg.io#grunt-contrib-sass) requires Ruby, and the Ruby Sass library, to be installed.

It should be noted that we also have the option of not using a preprocessor at all. In the next sections we will cover assets optimization, which can also be seen as a transform. So, even when using Vanilla JavaScript, CSS, and HTML, we find we still need Grunt to perform our optimizations.

Grunt in Action

Before we configure these plugins, let's first create and compile some source files. We will segregate our source files into three subdirectories: `scripts`, `styles`, and `views`. Note that these directory names are chosen because they are language agnostic. Once we have created each of these subdirectories inside our `src` directory, we then need to create an initial file in each, as below:

```
//Code example 02-project
// src/scripts/app.coffee
alert 'hello world'

// src/styles/app.styl
html, body
  margin 0
  padding 0

// src/views/app.jade
!!!5
html
  head
    link(rel="stylesheet", href="css/app.css")
  body
    h5 Hello World
    script(src="js/app.js")
```

> When placing our link tags (stylesheets) and script tags inside our HTML, it is best to place all of our link tags at the top, inside the `head` element, and to place all of our scripts at the very bottom, at the end of the `body` element. This causes browsers to load the stylesheets first, letting the user see a correctly styled version of the page while it is loading.

Now, inside our `Gruntfile.js` file, we will load the tasks provided by these plugins, then configure each to compile the corresponding `app` file from our `src` directory into our `build` directory:

```
//Code example 02-project
// Gruntfile.js
module.exports = function(grunt) {

  // Load tasks provided by each plugin
  grunt.loadNpmTasks("grunt-contrib-coffee");
  grunt.loadNpmTasks("grunt-contrib-stylus");
  grunt.loadNpmTasks("grunt-contrib-jade");

  // Project configuration
```

```
grunt.initConfig({
  coffee: {
    build: {
      src: "src/scripts/app.coffee",
      dest: "build/js/app.js"
    }
  },
  stylus: {
    build: {
      src: "src/styles/app.styl",
      dest: "build/css/app.css"
    }
  },
  jade: {
    build: {
      options: {
        pretty: true
      },
      src: "src/views/app.jade",
      dest: "build/app.html"
    }
  }
});
// Define the default task
grunt.registerTask('default', ['coffee','stylus','jade']);
};
```

At this point, our `project` directory should look like:

```
//Code example 02-project
project/
├── Gruntfile.js
├── node_modules
│   ├── grunt
│   ├── grunt-contrib-coffee
│   ├── grunt-contrib-jade
│   └── grunt-contrib-stylus
├── package.json
└── src
    ├── scripts
    │   └── app.coffee
    ├── styles
    │   └── app.styl
    └── views
        └── app.jade
```

Now we are ready to transpile our source files. Since we have aliased our default task to our `coffee`, `stylus`, and `jade` tasks, we can simply execute `grunt`, yielding:

```
$ grunt
Running "coffee:build" (coffee) task
File build/js/app.js created.

Running "stylus:build" (stylus) task
File build/css/app.css created.

Running "jade:build" (jade) task
File "build/app.html" created.

Done, without errors.
```

We should now have a new `build` directory that looks like:

```
build/
├── app.html
├── css
│   └── app.css
└── js
    └── app.js
```

This separation between our `src` and `build` directories is important, as the contents of `build` will be overwritten without warning. Therefore, it is clear that the source files are intended to be modified, whereas the build files are temporary. To further emphasize the latter, we should add our `build` directory to our version control system's ignore list. This will force the developer to run Grunt in order to generate the `build` directory and help new developers get used to the Grunt workflow. It also helps discover any bugs with the build.

Upon opening our newly generated `app.html` file, we should be greeted with the following window:

Step 3 – organizing our source files

In the previous step, we configured a one-to-one mapping for each task. In practice, however, we will want a more robust solution.

Scripts

Let's start with our CoffeeScript files, as mentioned in *Chapter 1, Introducing Grunt*, in the subsection on *Concatenation*. While it is important to separate functionality into individual files, it is also important to reduce the number of scripts included on the page. Both goals can be achieved through file concatenation. Let's now modify our `coffee` task's configuration to compile and concatenate all files within our scripts directory. Luckily, our `coffee` task allows us to select multiple source files, providing us with the ability to concatenate them into one file:

```
//Code example 03-project
coffee: {
  build: {
    options: {
      join: true
    },
    src: "src/scripts/**/*.coffee",
    dest: "build/js/app.js"
  }
}
```

Grunt in Action

> The `join` option tells the `coffee` task to concatenate before compiling; this is favorable, as we shall soon see. We can view examples, and a complete list of `coffee` task options, on `http://gswg.io#grunt-contrib-coffee` plugin's GitHub repository at `http://gswg.io#grunt-contrib-coffee`.

Instead of listing out individual files, the glob string `src/scripts/**/*.coffee` is used to match all CoffeeScript files within `scripts` and its subdirectories. To see this in action, we will add two utility functions, each in its own file:

```
//Code example 03-project
//src/scripts/util/add.coffee
add = (a, b) -> a + b
```

```
//src/scripts/util/subtract.coffee
subtract = (a, b) -> a - b
```

And we will also modify our `app.coffee` to make use of these functions:

```
//src/scripts/app.coffee
alert add 7, subtract 4, 1
```

Now, when we run our `coffee` task:

```
$ grunt coffee
Running "coffee:build" (coffee) task
File build/js/app.js created.

Done, without errors.
```

Then, display the resulting `build/js/app.js file`, we should see:

```
$ cat build/js/app.js
(function() {
  var add, subtract;

  alert(add(7, subtract(4, 1)));

  add = function(a, b) {
    return a + b;
  };

  subtract = function(a, b) {
    return a - b;
  };
}).call(this);
```

> The function wrapper around compiled code is known as an **Immediately-Invoked Function Expression (IIFE)**. By default, compiled CoffeeScript code is wrapped in an IIFE, which essentially makes our code private. This helps to separate our JavaScript from the rest of the JavaScript on the page, and is considered best practice. We can read more about this concept on Ben Alman's blog at http://gswg.io#iife. The join option, described previously, causes one IIFE to be placed around all of our files instead of wrapping each individual file.

In the above file, we notice our usage of add and subtract appears before they are defined. This will result in an error. We fix this by using an array in the coffee task's src property, and by explicitly placing app.coffee after the glob string to match all CoffeeScript files:

```
coffee: {
  build: {
    options: {
      join: true
    },
    src: [
      "src/scripts/**/*.coffee",
      "!src/scripts/app.coffee",
      "src/scripts/app.coffee"
    ],
    dest: "build/js/app.js"
  }
}
```

To achieve this in Grunt version 0.4.x, we must first exclude app.coffee from the file set (by prefixing the file path with an exclamation mark !), then re-include it. Running grunt coffee and displaying the result should now correctly yield:

```
$ grunt coffee
...
$ cat build/js/app.js
(function() {
  var add, subtract;
  add = function(a, b) {
    return a + b;
  };
  subtract = function(a, b) {
```

```
        return a - b;
    };

    alert(add(7, subtract(4, 1)));

}).call(this);
```

Now when we open our app.html file again, we should see the following window:

[Screenshot of a JavaScript Alert dialog in a "Hello World" window showing the number 10 with an OK button]

Even if we choose not to use CoffeeScript and just use JavaScript, there is still value in separating our files into individual pieces of functionality, then concatenating them together. This can be done using the grunt-contrib-concat plugin in a similar fashion. That is, in place of the coffee task configuration, we would insert this concat task configuration:

```
concat: {
  build: {
    src: [
      "src/scripts/**/*.js",
      "!src/scripts/app.js",
      "src/scripts/app.js"
    ],
    dest: "build/js/app.js"
  }
}
```

This technique allows us to freely create as many CoffeeScript (or JavaScript) files and subdirectories as we like. Then when we run `grunt`, all script files inside `src/scripts` will be merged into one file, `build/js/app.js`, which represents all of our application's JavaScript.

> For building cohesive single-page applications, I recommend using AngularJS (`http://gswg.io#angular`). A useful set of AngularJS tutorials (in screencast form) can be found at `http://gswg.io#angular-screencasts`. Next, I would recommend `Ember.js` (`http://gswg.io#ember`). Opposed to simply using jQuery, these frameworks provide a convention for structuring your JavaScript. This layout normalization of each project becomes a strong advantage, as each developer on the team knows where each portion of code should be.

Views

Next, we will give our views some structure. Here we use the term "view" as a language agnostic name for Jade code. As mentioned previously, in place of Jade we could also use Haml or EJS. Since we are building a single-page application, our `app.html` file is all we need, so our one-to-one compilation will suffice. However, we still want to avoid placing our entire application inside one file. In order to split our Jade code across multiple files, we will use the `include` directive. The Jade documentation on `include` (`http://gswg.io#jade-include`) describes how to statically include chunks of Jade, or other content such as CSS or HTML, which live in separate files. Below we shall make use of `include` by creating a logical separation of our single page. The structure of a single-page application can vary widely; however, in this example, we assume we have a header section, a content section, and a footer section. Instead of writing the code for each section inside our `app.jade` file, we will create a new `app` directory to house three new Jade files. Once complete, we should have the following `views` folder:

```
src/views
├── app
│   ├── content.jade
│   ├── footer.jade
│   └── header.jade
└── app.jade
```

Now we can make use of our new files inside our `app.jade` with the `include` directive:

```
!!!5
html
```

```
head
  link(rel="stylesheet", href="css/app.css")
body

  include app/header
  include app/content
  include app/footer

  script(src="js/app.js")
```

Running our `jade` task with `grunt jade` should leave us with the following `build/app.html` file:

```
<!DOCTYPE html>
<html>
  <head>
    <link rel="stylesheet" href="css/app.css">
  </head>
  <body>
    <section class="header">this is the <b>amazing</b> header section</section>
    <section class="content">
      <div class="top">some content with this on top</div>
      <div class="middle">and this in the middle</div>
      <div class="bottom">and this on the bottom</div>
    </section>
    <section class="footer">
      and this is the footer, with an awesome copyright
      symbol with the year next to it - &copy; 2013
    </section>
    <script src="js/app.js"></script>
  </body>
</html>
```

Instead of placing our new Jade files alongside `app.jade`, we have put them inside a new `app` directory. This is to prevent our `views` folder from becoming a large flat structure. By just looking at the file hierarchy we can see that `app.jade` contains `head.jade`, `content.jade`, and `footer.jade`.

Note: we could apply this idea again to our `content.jade`, inside our new `app` folder by making a `content` folder with more Jade files, each representing views inside `content.jade`. This small convention will assist us greatly when our application becomes a 20,000-line monster.

When our application begins to display the signs of monstrosity, we might wish to add more one-to-one compilations and then use **XMLHTTPRequest (XHR)** to asynchronously load the extra HTML as required. For example, Gmail might load the "mail" view initially, and then dynamically load the "contacts" view when the user navigates to the Gmail Contacts section. So, if we are writing a Gmail clone, our `app.html` file would become `mail.html` and then we'd also add a `contacts.html` file.

Styles

Now, let's move onto our styles. We could organize our styles in the same way as our scripts, by concatenating them all together using a "match all Stylus files" glob string, or we could use the Stylus directive: `@import`, which is similar to Jade's `include` directive. In this example, we will use the latter method. Though it may be less time consuming to simply match all Stylus files in one fell swoop, by explicitly defining which files are included, we can also choose where to include them. Using the `@import` directive nested within our style definitions, we can reset our file's indentation and avoid copious nesting. For example, we can do the following modifications:

```
//src/styles/app.styl
html, body
  margin 0
  padding 0

.content
  @import "app/content"

@media (max-width: 768px)
  .content
    @import "app/m-content"

//src/styles/app/content.styl
.middle
  //desktop font size
  font-size 16pt

//src/styles/app/m-content.styl
.middle
  //mobile font size
  font-size 8pt
```

Our `src/styles/app/content.styl` and `src/styles/app/m-content.styl` files contain our desktop and mobile overrides for our content section. Now, when we build our styles with `grunt stylus`, our `build/css/app.css` file should contain the following code:

```
html,
body {
  margin: 0;
  padding: 0;
}
.content .middle {
  font-size: 16pt;
}
@media (max-width: 768px) {
  .content .middle {
    font-size: 8pt;
  }
}
```

Also, using `@import`, we can include third party CSS frameworks such as Bootstrap or Foundation. We can inline CSS files wherever we desire by setting the `include css` option to `true` and by `@import`ing a CSS file instead of a Stylus file. For example at the top of our `app.styl` we could do `@import "vendor/bootstrap.css"`.

Step 4 – optimizing our build files

At this point, we should have a structured set of source files and can now perform additional transformations on the result. Let's start by downloading the plugins from npm and saving them in our `package.json` file:

```
$ npm install --save-dev grunt-contrib-uglify grunt-contrib-cssmin grunt-contrib-htmlmin
```

Then, at the top of our `Gruntfile.js` file, where we have loaded our other Grunt plugins, we will load our new additions with:

```
grunt.loadNpmTasks("grunt-contrib-uglify");
grunt.loadNpmTasks("grunt-contrib-cssmin");
grunt.loadNpmTasks("grunt-contrib-htmlmin");
```

Scripts

We will start by compressing our scripts. In this example, we use the `grunt-contrib-uglify` plugin (http://gswg.io#grunt-contrib-uglify), which is a wrapper around the popular UglifyJS library (http://gswg.io#uglifyjs). Now we have loaded the plugin, which provides the `uglify` task, we just need to configure it:

```
uglify: {
  compress: {
    src: "<%= coffee.build.dest %>",
    dest: "<%= coffee.build.dest %>"
  }
}
```

Here, inside the `uglify` property, we have made a `compress` target, which has `src` and `dest` set to the same file. Instead of entering the actual filename, we are making use of Grunt templates to retrieve the value at the given configuration path (`coffee.build.dest`), which in this case, resolves to `build/js/app.js`. Grunt templates make it easy to have a single source of truth within our configuration. Therefore, if we ever want to change the file path of our JavaScript, we only need to change one configuration entry.

Since we have set the source and destination to the same file path, in effect, we are overwriting our JavaScript with the compressed version of itself. However, if we were writing a JavaScript library instead of a web application, we'd most likely want to compress our `app.js` file into an `app.min.js` file, so its users could download an uncompressed and a compressed version.

> Review the Grunt templates in *Chapter 2, Setting Up Grunt*, or visit the Grunt website at http://gswg.io#grunt-templates.

Running this `uglify` task with this basic configuration should result in the following `app.js` file:

```
(function(){var a,b;a=function(a,b){return a+b},b=function(a,b){return a-b},alert(a(7,b(4,1)))}).call(this);
```

Generally, this will suffice, however, `UglifyJS` also offers advanced features. For example, in some cases, we might have portions of code that are only used during development. We could remove this unnecessary code with the following technique. By defining a `DEBUG` variable and place our debug-related code inside an `if` block as follows:

```
if(DEBUG) {
  //do things here
}
```

Then, if we used the following `options` object inside our `uglify` configuration as follows:

```
options: {
  compress: {
    global_defs: {
      "DEBUG": false
    },
    dead_code: true
  }
}
```

This would result in `UglifyJS` locking the value of `DEBUG` to `false` and also to remove the inaccessible code (dead code). Therefore, in addition to compressing code, we also have the ability to completely remove code from our builds. The documentation for this feature can be found at http://gswg.io#grunt-contrib-uglify-conditional-compilation.

Styles

To compress our styles, we use the `grunt-contrib-cssmin` plugin (http://gswg.io#grunt-contrib-cssmin), which is a wrapper around the `clean-css` library (http://gswg.io#clean-css). Since we have installed this plugin, we just need to include the `cssmin` task configuration:

```
cssmin: {
  compress: {
    src: "<%= stylus.build.dest %>",
    dest: "<%= stylus.build.dest %>"
  }
}
```

Similar to our scripts configuration, we can see that the only real difference is that we point to the `stylus` task's output instead of pointing to the `coffee` task's output. When we run `grunt cssmin`, our `css/app.css` file should be modified to the following one:

```
html,body{margin:0;padding:0}.content .middle{font-size:16pt}@media
(max-width:768px){.content .middle{font-size:8pt}}
```

Views

Finally, to compress our views, we will use the `grunt-contrib-htmlmin` plugin (http://gswg.io#grunt-contrib-htmlmin), which is a wrapper around the `html-minifier` library (http://gswg.io#html-minifier). The `htmlmin` configuration has a little more to it: since its compression options are disabled by default, we need to enable the rules we wish to use:

```
htmlmin: {
  options: {
    removeComments: true,
    collapseWhitespace: true,
    collapseBooleanAttributes: true,
    removeAttributeQuotes: true,
    removeRedundantAttributes: true,
    removeOptionalTags: true
  },
  compress: {
    src: "<%= jade.build.dest %>",
    dest: "<%= jade.build.dest %>"
  }
}
```

Now our `htmlmin` task is configured, we can run it with `grunt htmlmin`, which should modify our `build/app.html` to the following:

```
<!DOCTYPE html><html><head><link rel=stylesheet href=css/app.
css><body><section class=header>this is the <b>amazing</b> header
section</section><section class=content><div class=top>some content
with this on top</div><div class=middle>and this in the middle</
div><div class=bottom>and this on the bottom</div></section><section
class=footer>and this is the footer, with an awesome copyright symbol
with the year next to it - &copy; 2013</section><script src=js/app.
js></script>
```

> In addition to the GitHub repository, we can read more about `html-minifier` on Juriy "Kangax" Zaytsev's blog at http://gswg.io#experimenting-with-html-minifier.

Step 5 – tasks and options

Currently, we have the tasks our plugins have provided and our `default` task, which runs our `coffee`, `stylus`, and `jade` tasks. We could extend our `default` task to include our optimizer tasks, but this would make debugging harder as our source code would always be minified. We can solve this programmatic creation of task aliases as follows:

```
// Initialize environment
var env = grunt.option('env') || 'dev';

// Environment specific tasks
if(env === 'prod') {
  grunt.registerTask('scripts', ['coffee', 'uglify']);
  grunt.registerTask('styles',  ['stylus', 'cssmin']);
  grunt.registerTask('views',   ['jade',   'htmlmin']);
} else {
  grunt.registerTask('scripts', ['coffee']);
  grunt.registerTask('styles',  ['stylus']);
  grunt.registerTask('views',   ['jade']);
}

// Define the default task
grunt.registerTask('default', ['scripts','styles','views']);
```

Here, we are initializing our current environment with a default value of development (`dev`), and then we are grouping our existing tasks into our three groups: `scripts`, `styles`, and `views`. If the value of our environment option (`env`) is set to production (`prod`), we will include our optimizer tasks for each group; otherwise it will run only the build tasks.

Instead of defining different sets of aliases, we could achieve the same result by defining custom tasks for `scripts`, `styles`, and `views`, and then within the task function, we could perform our environment check and programmatically run the tasks we desire. For example, we could write the task function for our `scripts` like:

```
grunt.registerTask('scripts', function() {
  grunt.task.run ('coffee');
```

```
    if(env === 'prod') {
      grunt.task.run('uglify');
    }
  });
```

As our build grows, it may become beneficial to use a custom task function. Nevertheless, in this instance, we will use the former method for simplicity.

Also, we are using the concept of environments. For example, while debugging our single-page application on our local machine, we will want to include the complete source and also want our debug code enabled. Then, when we are ready to test, we most likely will want to optimize our source to simulate production, but keep our debug code enabled, so our testers can report bugs with ease.

Finally, when the time comes to deploy our single-page application to production, we will still want to optimize our code, but also disable our debug code so our users don't see cryptic error messages. Therefore, instead of using options such as `--optimize` and `--enable-debug` and including them or not including them for various builds, we will simply use an `--env` option and modify our build based on the value of the environment.

> Unfortunately we can't use `--debug` as a run-time option as it's already used by Grunt to enable `task` debugging during our builds.

Let's give our new, environment-driven build a try:

```
$ grunt
Running "coffee:build" (coffee) task
File build/js/app.js created.

Running "stylus:build" (stylus) task
File build/css/app.css created.

Running "jade:build" (jade) task
File "build/app.html" created.

Done, without errors.
```

Here, we can see that our build is the same by default, however, when we set our environment to production by including the command-line argument `--env=prod`, we should see the following result:

```
$ grunt --env=prod
Running "coffee:build" (coffee) task
File build/js/app.js created.

Running "uglify:compress" (uglify) task
File "build/js/app.js" created.

Running "stylus:build" (stylus) task
File build/css/app.css created.

Running "cssmin:compress" (cssmin) task
File build/css/app.css created.

Running "jade:build" (jade) task
File "build/app.html" created.

Running "htmlmin:compress" (htmlmin) task
File build/app.html created.

Done, without errors.
```

Step 6 – improving development flow

As developers, in order to stay productive during the day, it's important to be "in the zone". In psychology, this concept is known as flow (http://gswg.io#flow); many people write about it (http://gswg.io#blog-on-flow) and many people talk about it (http://gswg.io#talk-on-flow). For instance, instead of editing our code and going back to the command line and running the appropriate tasks, we can make use of the watch task provided by the grunt-contrib-watch plugin (http://gswg.io#grunt-contrib-watch). The watch task allows us to specify a set of files to "watch" and a set of tasks to run when they change. Let's get started by installing the grunt-contrib-watch plugin:

```
$ npm install --save-dev grunt-contrib-watch
```

Once that's completed, we will register the `watch` task by loading the `grunt-contrib-watch` plugin with the following code:

```
grunt.loadNpmTasks("grunt-contrib-watch");
```

We will add this line below our other calls to `grunt.loadNpmTasks`. Next, we configure the `watch` task to run our `scripts` task whenever we change one of our script files (a CoffeeScript file in this instance), and then the equivalent for `styles` (Stylus files) and `views` (Jade files):

```
watch: {
  scripts: {
    files: "src/scripts/**/*.coffee",
    tasks: "scripts"
  },
  styles: {
    files: "src/styles/**/*.styl",
    tasks: "styles"
  },
  views: {
    files: "src/views/**/*.jade",
    tasks: "views"
  }
}
```

In addition to this, we extend our `default` task to include the `watch` task:

```
grunt.registerTask('build', ['scripts','styles','views']);
// Define the default task
grunt.registerTask('default', ['build','watch']);
```

Notice that we moved the original three tasks into their own `build` task. Although this does change the build's behavior, it makes it more comprehensible. By default, we will build then watch. Our build is now ready; let's give it a try:

```
$ grunt
Running "coffee:build" (coffee) task
File build/js/app.js created.

Running "stylus:build" (stylus) task
File build/css/app.css created.

Running "jade:build" (jade) task
File "build/app.html" created.
```

```
Running "watch" task
Waiting...
OK
>> File "src/views/app/footer.jade" changed.

Running "jade:build" (jade) task
File "build/app.html" created.

Done, without errors.
Completed in 1.074s
Waiting...
OK
>> File "src/scripts/app.coffee" changed.

Running "coffee:build" (coffee) task
File build/js/app.js created.

Done, without errors.
Completed in 0.782s
Waiting...
```

First, we ran grunt. This ran our usual build followed by our new watch task. This caused build to wait for file changes. Then, we saved our src/views/app/footer.jade file and our watch task detected this change and ran the views task. Finally, we edited src/scripts/app.coffee file and our watch task similarly ran the scripts task in response.

So, instead of returning to the command line every few minutes, we can stay inside our code editor and preview it with a browser window alongside.

> We can take this even further by automating browser refreshes on file changes with **LiveReload**. The grunt-contrib-watch plugin provides this functionality via the livereload option (http://gswg.io#watch-livereload), then instead of adding the LiveReload script to all of our pages, we can simply use the LiveReload Chrome extension (http://gswg.io#chrome-livereload).

Step 7 – deploying our application

At this point, we are able to build and optionally optimize our source files into three files build/js/app.js, build/css/app.css, and build/index.html. Now we are ready to deploy our single-page application. In this example, we deploy to Amazon's **Simple Storage Service (S3)** using the grunt-aws Grunt plugin (http://gswg.io#grunt-aws). First, we install the plugin as follows:

```
$ npm install --save-dev grunt-aws
```

We now load the plugin, which will provide the s3 task:

```
grunt.loadNpmTasks("grunt-aws");
```

Next, similar to a previous example in *Chapter 1, Introducing Grunt*, on deployment, we configure the s3 task to deploy the entire contents of our build to a jpillora-app-<env> bucket, where env is set to the current environment:

```
aws: grunt.file.readJSON("aws.json"),
s3: {
  options: {
    accessKeyId: "<%= aws.accessKeyId %>",
    secretAccessKey: "<%= aws.secretAccessKey %>",
    bucket: "jpillora-app-"+env
  },
  build: {
    cwd: "build/",
    src: "**"
  }
}
```

Before defining our s3 property, we define an aws property and initialize it with our **Amazon Web Services (AWS)** credentials, which are loaded from an external JSON file: aws.json. Inside our s3 configuration, we are setting the bucket option based on the environment (env) variable set in the previous section. Next, we are creating a target called build, which represents the deployment of our build. Our build target is defining a set of source (src) files to upload; however, we are using the build/ directory as our current working directory (cwd). In effect, we are uploading the contents of the build/ directory into the root directory of our bucket. Finally, we create a deploy task that aliases build and then s3; this way we can always be sure we are deploying the current build:

```
grunt.registerTask('deploy',['build', 's3']);
```

In practice, we will most likely want to deploy our application to a staging (or testing) environment to allow our **Quality assurance** (**QA**) team to verify that our latest deployment functions as expected. Therefore, once we create our bucket, we can use `grunt deploy --env=test` to deploy our single-page application to our `jpillora-app-test` bucket:

```
$ grunt deploy --env=test
Running "coffee:build" (coffee) task...
Running "stylus:build" (stylus) task...
Running "jade:build" (jade) task...

Running "s3:build" (s3) task
Retrieving list of existing objects...
>> Put 'app.html'
>> Put 'css/app.css'
>> Put 'js/app.js'
>> Put 3 files
```

Currently, setting our environment (`env`) to `test` has no effect except for the destination bucket, so when we visit this recent deployment at `http://gswg.io#jpillora-app-test`, we should see our default build. However, we could vary our build steps for `test`. For example, we could enable error reporting or add a testing console into the page for the QA team. Once we are given the green light to deploy to production, we will simply use `grunt deploy --env=prod`, which should yield the following result:

```
$ grunt deploy --env=prod
Running "coffee:build" (coffee) task...
Running "uglify:compress" (uglify) task...
Running "stylus:build" (stylus) task...
Running "cssmin:compress" (cssmin) task...
Running "jade:build" (jade) task...
Running "htmlmin:compress" (htmlmin) task...

Running "s3:build" (s3) task
Retrieving list of existing objects...
>> Put 'app.html'
>> Put 'js/app.js'
>> Put 'css/app.css'
>> Put 3 files
```

This time, we built and optimized our source code, and then most importantly, uploaded the result into the production bucket, which can be viewed at http://gswg.io#jpillora-app-prod. We can verify this by visiting both pages and ensuring test is just our usual build, whereas prod should also be optimized.

The grunt-aws plugin provides **gzip** compression before each upload and caches the hash of each file so bandwidth is not wasted uploading the same file multiple times. Also, grunt-aws allows us to change the region, set custom headers, and much more.

Summary

In conclusion, we should now be able to set up a new Grunt environment from the start, install and load a set of desired plugins, then configure them to achieve a given result. This chapter uses the concept of a single-page application; however, these same concepts could be applied to a multipage website. In the next chapter, we will briefly cover some advanced topics directly and indirectly related to Grunt, such as *Testing with Grunt*, *Advanced Grunt*, *Advanced JavaScript*, and *Development Tools*.

5
Advanced Grunt

Up until now, this book has covered the core concepts required to effectively use Grunt. In this chapter, we shall blaze through some extra ideas, plugins, and tools to take our front-end development to the next level. We will get a sneak peak into *Testing with Grunt*, *Continuous integration with Grunt*, *External tasks*, and *Grunt plugins*. Finally, we will review a series of *JavaScript resources* and *developer tools*.

Testing with Grunt

Performing automated tests is another major use case for Grunt. Let us say our build process involves compiling, analyzing, optimizing, and then deploying our application. This sequential nature of Grunt is useful because if any link in the above process fails, Grunt will not proceed, that is, any subsequent tasks will not be run. This is important because it prevents our analysis tasks from running when our build tasks fail to create the files that we need to analyze. However, static analysis won't spot logical errors in our build files, therefore we may still be deploying a buggy application despite a successful build. We can work towards preventing this by including a test suite to our application –placing our new `test` task *before* our `deploy` task. Even if we have a **Quality Assurance** (QA) team, which manually tests our application, using a test suite can save QA iterations by quickly catching logic errors.

A test suite is also useful for trapping regression errors. Our QA team might spend weeks testing our application, however, after a number of development iterations without a test suite, they are forced to go back and perform the same tests again to ensure our new code has not broken old functionality. Therefore, our whole team's development cycle can be improved by implementing effective automated tests.

Advanced Grunt

There are a wide variety of JavaScript testing frameworks available, however, the two most popular frameworks are **Jasmine** and **Mocha**. Mocha (http://gswg.io#mocha) was written by *TJ Holowaychuk*, the prolific developer who also brought us Jade, Stylus, and Express. Mocha has one of the widest feature sets across all testing frameworks, with first class support for asynchronous APIs. Below is a simple test written using Mocha's **Behavior Driven Design (BDD)** syntax:

```
//Code Example 01-testing
// test/array-tests.js
describe('Array', function(){
  describe('#indexOf()', function(){
    it('should return -1 when not in the array', function(){
      expect([1,2,3].indexOf(5)).to.equal(-1);
      expect([1,2,3].indexOf(0)).to.equal(-1);
    });
  });
});
```

Here we can see the BDD syntax entails a `describe` and an `it` function:

- `describe` is used to create a named container (or namespace) for individual tests. These containers are conveyed when we run the test suite to help us see what kinds of tests are passing and failing.
- `it` is used to define a test. This function accepts a string of our choice, which states one behavior that should hold true, for example, `it("should do foo and bar", …)`.

In addition to Mocha, we have included the Chai assertion library (http://gswg.io#chai) which allows us to make use of its `expect` function—a function used to perform assertions and throw appropriate errors for Mocha to catch.

In `Code Example 01-testing`, we are using the Grunt plugin `grunt-mocha` (http://gswg.io#grunt-mocha) to run Mocha in a headless browser called **PhantomJS** (http://gswg.io#phantomjs). PhantomJS is a Web browser without the user interface. This API-only browser is programmable, which allows it to communicate with Grunt via a plugin. Let us give `Code Example 01-testing` a try:

```
$ grunt
Running "mocha:test" (mocha) task
Testing: test/runner.html

  1 test complete (2 ms)
>> 1 passed! (0.00s)
Done, without errors.
```

We can see `grunt-mocha` is testing our `test/runner.html`, and we have a reference to our simple `test/array-tests.js` file, which provides one test case. When run, we should see green or red dots for each test passed or failed. In this example, we have one green dot for our single passed test case. However, if we open `test/runner.html` in a Web browser, instead of Grunt (PhantomJS), we should see Mocha's built-in test reporter. An example of Mocha's browser test runner can be found at `http://gswg.io#mocha-browser-example`.

Since Grunt is mainly used for front-end Web development, we have used Mocha to test browser JavaScript code. However, Mocha can also be used to test Node.js JavaScript code.

Effective testing methods in JavaScript is a large topic, so this short introduction should gives us an idea of how tests look, and how we can use Grunt to integrate a test step into our builds.

Continuous integration with Grunt

To put it simply, a continuous integration (or CI) server is a dedicated machine with the sole purpose of running builds, that is, it will continuously integrate the new build into a given system. Generally, CI servers work by creating an HTTP server and listening for data to be sent to it. Then, HTTP clients can post data to this server, triggering the server to start the build. For instance, you could tell GitHub to trigger your CI server on every commit (`http://gswg.io#github-webhooks`), then use Grunt on your CI to continuously perform tasks (such as analyzing, compiling, testing, and deploying your build) as new code arrives. When set up correctly, the act of committing to the main branch in your repository could analyze, compile, test, and deploy your application. This streamlined approach to deployment is highly valuable as it reduces development iteration time. See this Wikipedia page for a list of continuous integration servers `http://gswg.io#ci-list`.

External tasks

In many instances, our `Gruntfile.js` file can become quite large and complicated, especially when we start including our own custom tasks into the mix. Grunt provides the means to split our custom tasks into their own individual files, thereby reducing the complexity of our `Gruntfile.js` and increasing reusability, since this new task file could also be used in other Grunt projects. In *Chapter 3*, *Using Grunt*, we learnt how to use `grunt.registerTask` to create our own custom tasks; however, to move these calls to `registerTask` into another file, we will need a reference to the `grunt` object (since `grunt` is passed into our `Gruntfile.js`).

Advanced Grunt

This is exactly what the `grunt.loadTasks` function does: it is called with a directory path as the argument, then runs every JavaScript file inside the given directory as if it were a "mini" `Gruntfile.js` file (also passing it the current `grunt` object). The following example demonstrates this:

```
//Code example 02-external-tasks
// Gruntfile.js
module.exports = function(grunt) {
  grunt.loadTasks("./tasks");
  grunt.initConfig({
    foo: {
      bar: 42
    }
  });
  grunt.registerTask("default", ["foo"]);
};
// tasks/foo.js
module.exports =function(grunt) {
  grunt.registerTask("foo", function() {
    console.log("foo says bar is: " + grunt.config("foo.bar"));
  });

};
```

In the example above, we are defining the `foo` task in a `foo.js` file, *inside* a `tasks` directory. In addition to `foo.js`, we could include as many other JavaScript files as we like and perform anything that we could do in our `Gruntfile.js`.

Grunt plugins

With the concepts from the section above, it becomes easy to understand how Grunt plugins work. Grunt plugins are just normal Node.js modules (that is, any directory with a `package.json` file), with the addition that they contain a `tasks` directory with JavaScript files to load. As we have seen throughout this book, when we wish to load the tasks provided by a Grunt plugin, we call the `grunt.loadNpmTasks` function with the name of the module. This `loadNpmTasks` function is very similar to the `loadTasks` function described previously, however, instead of using a directory to find JavaScript files, it uses the name of a module and then looks inside that module for a `tasks` folder. Therefore, the following two lines are equivalent:

```
//Code example 03-load-plugin
grunt.loadNpmTasks("grunt-contrib-copy");
grunt.loadTasks("./node_modules/grunt-contrib-copy/tasks");
```

Now, with this in mind, if we want to create *and share* our own tasks, we can publish them as a plugin. All we need to do is:

1. Write a custom task with `registerTask`.
2. Place it in a file inside a `tasks` directory.
3. Create a new `package.json` file alongside this `tasks` directory.
4. Finally, publish it to npm with `npm publish`.

In short, this is all we need to do to share a Grunt plugin publicly. However, we will go through each step carefully and add a few extra steps to make it more accessible for others.

First, let us write our custom task and place it in a new `tasks` directory:

```
//Code Example 04-sample-plugin
// tasks/gswg.js
module.exports = function(grunt) {

  grunt.registerTask("gswg", function() {
    grunt.log.ok("Hello, you have successfully run
                  the 'gswg' task.");
  });

};
```

We will notice that we have named our new task file `gswg.js` (since it is providing the `gswg` task), though it looks like a `Gruntfile.js`. As mentioned previously, `loadTasks` will run each file as if it were a "mini" `Gruntfile.js` – allowing us to extend the `Gruntfile.js` that called `loadTasks`.

> Grunt provides an API for creating various types of log messages. The Grunt API documentation contains information on `grunt.log`, which can be found at `http://gswg.io#grunt-log`.

Next, we will create our `package.json`. We can create it manually or with `npm init`. In order for npm to accept our module, it *requires* two fields: `name` and `version`. So in this example, we will give it the `name` of `grunt-gswg` and we will give it the initial `version` of `0.1.0`. Also note that we have prefixed our module name with `grunt-` so that Grunt users can recognize this as a Grunt plugin.

Advanced Grunt

In addition to these two required fields, we will also tell npm that our module is a plugin (or extension) for the `grunt` module using the `peerDependencies` property. Although we could use the `dependencies` property, doing so would cause every Grunt plugin to each install its own copy of the `grunt` module. The `peerDependencies` property solves this by using the parent module's `node_modules` directory, instead of the current module's `node_modules` directory.

To allow our module to be seen as a Grunt plugin, we will also need to add a `keywords` array property and include `"gruntplugin"`. The `keywords` array lists search terms that help npm users find modules. For instance, if we made a Grunt plugin to create a copy of a database, we might also include `"copy"`, `"clone"`, `"replicate"`, `"database"`, and `"db"`. This will allow users to find our plugin even if they use an assortment of equivalent search terms.

To finalize our `package.json`, we will also include:

- An `author` property, containing our contact information. In this case, I have used `"Jaime Pillora <gswg@jpillora.com>"`.
- A `license` property, specifying the software license that we wish to apply to our module. In this case, we will use `"MIT"`, which states that our module is free for everyone to use in any way.
- A `homepage` property, providing the URL to where our users can find out more about our module.

At this point, our `package.json` file now should look like:

```
{
  "name": "grunt-gswg",
  "version": "0.1.0",
  "author": "Jaime Pillora <gswg@jpillora.com>",
  "homepage": "https://github.com/jpillora/gswg-
              examples/tree/master/5/04-sample-plugin",
  "peerDependencies": {
    "grunt": "~0.4.0"
  },
  "keywords": [
    "gruntplugin",
    "example",
    "sample",
    "gswg"
  ],
  "license": "MIT"
}
```

Now that we have our new `gswg` task and a valid `package.json` file, we are able to publish to npm. Before we do, however, let us do some housekeeping. There is no point in publishing code for everyone to use if there is no documentation informing them of *how* to use it. So let us create a `README.md` file, which will inform users of the tasks this plugin provides, and the options that each task has available. This file is in the **Markdown** file format, which we can read more about here: `http://gswg.io#markdown`. We can find the `README.md` file for this example in the `Code Example 04-sample-plugin` directory.

At this point, we have created enough code to warrant a backup. Let us place our code into a version control system, like Git. It is important to have a navigable history of our plugin's modification history so we can restore old code if it gets deleted, and so when we would like to collaborate with others, there is the ability to branch and merge our code. In this example, let us commit what we have so far into GitHub. To create a new Git repository on GitHub, we will need to:

- Create a GitHub (`http://gswg.io#github`) account and sign in.
- Click the **Create New Repository** icon in the top-right hand corner.
- Use the plugin name as the repository name, and provide a short description, and click **Create Repository**.
- We will be taken to our new empty repository, where we will find instructions on how to set up this repository locally, and make our first commit.

> To learn more about using Git, and how to make the most of it, visit this page: `http://gswg.io#git-resources`.

Before we publish our plugin for general use, we want be sure that it works. As mentioned previously, it is best to create an automated test suite, which confirms our desired functionality is indeed *functional*. For this sample plugin, however, we will just use a dummy `Gruntfile.js` file and manually confirm that it works. Our plugin's users can also view this file as an example of our plugin in action.

We will start by creating a `Gruntfile.js` inside an `example` directory:

```
//Code Example 04-sample-plugin
// example/Gruntfile.js
module.exports = function(grunt) {
  grunt.loadTasks("../tasks");
  grunt.registerTask("default", ["gswg"]);
};
```

Advanced Grunt

Here, we are replicating `loadNpmTasks` by using `loadTasks` and directly referencing our `tasks` folder. Before we can run this `Gruntfile.js`, however, it will need the `grunt` module installed. Since we are using the `peerDependencies` property, we will also need to use the `devDependencies` property to tell npm to install `grunt` for local testing. So we will first use the following command:

```
$ npm install --save-dev grunt
```

Then we can run our dummy `Gruntfile.js` with:

```
$ cd example
$ grunt
Running "gswg" task
>> Hello, you have successfully run the 'gswg' task.

Done, without errors.
```

As we can see, our `gswg` task has run successfully and we are now ready to publish it. Now let us login to npm with `npm adduser`. This command is both login and account creation. It will give us three prompts: `name`, `email`, and `password`. Once we are logged in, we can enter `npm publish` and we should see:

```
$ npm publish
npm http PUT https://registry.npmjs.org/grunt-gswg
npm http 201 https://registry.npmjs.org/grunt-gswg
npm http GET https://registry.npmjs.org/grunt-gswg
npm http 200 https://registry.npmjs.org/grunt-gswg
npm http PUT https://registry.npmjs.org/grunt-gswg/-/grunt-gswg-0.1.0.tgz/-rev/1-0d89dbcc01a9b9d154a7f43bc103c411
npm http 201 https://registry.npmjs.org/grunt-gswg/-/grunt-gswg-0.1.0.tgz/-rev/1-0d89dbcc01a9b9d154a7f43bc103c411
npm http PUT https://registry.npmjs.org/grunt-gswg/0.1.0/-tag/latest
npm http 201 https://registry.npmjs.org/grunt-gswg/0.1.0/-tag/latest
+ grunt-gswg@0.1.0
```

This sample plugin has now been published to npm, which we can confirm with the `npm info grunt-gswg` command.

Useful plugins

Below is a list of Grunt plugins which, though not absolutely necessary, are very useful at times:

- *Running Grunt tasks concurrently*: `http://gswg.io#grunt-concurrent` with the `grunt-concurrent` plugin we can create groups of tasks which will run independently of each other, resulting in a faster build.
- *Load all Grunt plugins automatically*: `http://gswg.io#load-grunt-tasks` with the `load-grunt-tasks` plugin, you can replace all occurrences of `grunt.loadNpmTask(...);` with the single line, `require('load-grunt-tasks')(grunt);`. This function searches through our `package.json`'s `devDependency` field and automatically calls `grunt.loadNpmTask` for each module prefixed with `grunt`.
- *Run a basic fileserver with Grunt*: `http://gswg.io#grunt-contrib-connect` in some cases, we will be building the frontend portion of a Web Application or website without the backend serving our files. With the `grunt-contrib-connect` plugin, we can run our own simple fileserver on the port of our choice. This plugin works well with the `grunt-contrib-watch` plugin, as it allows us to run our build and locally serve our newly built files at the same time, all within Grunt.

JavaScript resources

The Web continues to evolve due to the forward march of standards and browsers. As browsers introduce new features, we can see the browser becoming a pseudo operating system, complete with access to hardware and the filesystem. When deciding between a native desktop application and a web application, our uses must be taken into consideration. With the universality and power of the browser, combined with ease of access, the decision is a simple one. The future is in web applications, driven by JavaScript. Here is a list of useful resources, for the JavaScript journeyman, to the JavaScript elite:

- *Mozilla Developer Network* (Everyone) `http://gswg.io#mdn` the Mozilla Developer Network is a great resource for all things in frontend development. It contains documentation for nearly every browser API, for both legacy and modern features.
- *Code Academy* (Beginner) `http://gswg.io#codeacademy` for an interactivity-based JavaScript learning experience, Code Academy has built a web application purely for teaching programming to prospective developers.
- *Eloquent JavaScript* (Beginner) `http://gswg.io#eloquent-javascript` in addition to being a great introduction to the JavaScript programming language, it is also a great book on programming in general. The author, *Marijn Haverbeke*, has kindly published Eloquent JavaScript online in HTML format under a Creative Commons license. Since the HTML version is displayed in a browser (which has a JavaScript engine), he has included runnable and editable code examples, which you can experiment with as you read.

- *JavaScript: The Good Parts* (Intermediate) `http://gswg.io#the-good-parts` regarded as "The JavaScript Bible" by some, The Good Parts discusses the history of JavaScript, and the good and the bad parts of JavaScript. This book is targeted at the intermediate developer who wishes to gain a deeper knowledge of language. The author, *Douglas Crockford*, has also given some great talks covering various topics from the book which can be found at `http://gswg.io#crockford-on-javascript`.
- *Learning JavaScript Design Patterns* (Advanced) `http://gswg.io#javascript-design-patterns` this Creative Commons book by *Addy Osmani* is targeted at professional developers wishing to improve their knowledge of design patterns and how they can be applied to the JavaScript programming language.

> Once you've been through these books and resources, you can visit `http://gswg.io#js-books`, where an organized and sortable list of JavaScript books is maintained.

Development tools

In this section, we will go over a selection of development tools, which directly and indirectly relate to the average Grunt development workflow.

Author picks

In this section, I will cover the tools of my own development environment, and the reasons why I think each is useful.

Mac OS X

In my opinion, Mac OS X (`http://gswg.io#osx`) provides the optimal development environment. Mac OS X combines a Unix-based operating system with a brilliant user experience, allowing you to make use of the vast number of Unix-based development tools without having to worry about system level intricacies and incompatibilities. **Homebrew** (`http://gswg.io#brew`) is an OS X alternative to Linux's `apt-get`, providing a simple and easy-to-use method for installing command-line tools.

Windows is useful if you develop on the Microsoft stack (.NET, C#, and so on). However, Mac OS X is better suited to frontend development. Since, in addition to Unix developer tools, there are many powerful graphics and design tools. If Mac OS X were not available, my next choice would the popular flavor of Linux, Ubuntu.

Sublime Text

Windows/Mac/Linux (`http://gswg.io#sublime`) for those who prefer the lighter weight of a text editor opposed to an **Integrated Development Environment (IDE)**, Sublime Text is the perfect choice. Due to its vast extendibility, a simple package manager was made called Package Control (`http://gswg.io#sublime-package-control`). Useful packages include:

- `SublimeLinter`—a multi-language static analyzer "linter", which displays code warnings inline as you type
- `CoffeeScript`/`Jade`/`Stylus`/`nginx`—an array of plugins providing syntax highlighting for the respective languages

SourceTree

Windows/Mac (`http://gswg.io#sourcetree`)— a clean user interface for Git, providing a faster means to visualize the current state of your Git repositories. Also, these visualizations lower the learning curve for beginners by clearly conveying Git concepts like branching and merging. SourceTree also includes **Git Flow** integration. Git Flow helps to enforce Git best practice by guiding your Git workflow.

Chrome DevTools

Windows/Mac/Linux (`http://gswg.io#chrome-devtools`)—Google Chrome's Developer Tools provides an extremely useful set of debugging, inspection, and performance analysis tools for all aspects of frontend development. There is also a Chrome DevTools extension called **Grunt DevTools** (`http://gswg.io#grunt-devtools`), which adds a "Grunt" tab inside Chrome DevTools, providing a user interface for Grunt.

Community picks

In this short section, we will review two popular tools used by the frontend community.

WebStorm

JetBrains (`http://gswg.io#webstorm`), creators of IntelliJ and RubyMine, also have an **IDE** for Web development. Similar to Sublime Text, there is a package manager with many useful plugins available.

Yeoman

Yeoman is a scaffolding tool (http://gswg.io#yeoman) used to generate projects using the current industry best practice, and also a workflow that utilizes Grunt and Twitter's Bower. The large community uptake of this tool has yielded code generators for many frameworks. For instance, there are code generators for constructing directives in Angular, models in Backbone, Ember components, and much more.

Summary

In this chapter, we have taken a brief look at JavaScript testing and a Grunt plugin, which we could use to integrate Mocha into our Grunt build. We have seen a short introduction into Grunt plugins and how they work, as well as other useful plugins. Finally, we covered JavaScript Resources and Development Tools not specifically related to Grunt, however, when combined with Grunt, each tool may help to bring our development cycle to the next level.

Thank you for purchasing Getting Started with Grunt: The JavaScript Task Runner. I hope this introduction to Grunt was both informative and interesting to read. You can find me on GitHub `http://gswg.io#jpillora` *and you may send comments and feedback to* `gswg@jpillora.com` *or tweet them at* `@jpillora`*. I look forward to hearing your responses.*

Index

Symbols

--save-dev option 41
--save option 41

A

Abstract Syntax Tree (AST) 47
Application Programming Interface (API) 43
args function 56
async function 56, 62
asynchronous tasks 61, 62
author property 106

B

Behavior Driven Design (BDD) syntax
  about 102
  describe function 102
  it function 102
build, creating
  application, deploying 97, 98
  build files, optimizing 88-90
  configuration, initial 76-80
  development flow, improving 94-96
  directory setup, initial 76
  source files, organizing 81-86
  tasks 92, 93
build files
  optimizing 88
build files, optimizing
  scripts 89, 90
  styles 90
  views 91
build tool 7

C

Chrome DevTools 111
Code Academy 109
CoffeeScript
  about 16, 17
  Haml 20
  Jade 17, 18
  LESS 20
  Sass 20
  Stylus 19
command-line
  about 62-64
  runtime options 66, 67
  task arguments 65, 66
  task, help 67, 68
Command line interface (CLI) 37
CommonJS
  about 31
  sample code 32
concatenation 21-23
consoleCheck task 46
Content Management Systems (CMS) 75
continuous integration (CI) 103
curly 14
cwd 53

D

data 60
describe function 102
dest 53
dest property 51
devDependencies property 108
development tools
  about 110

Author Picks 110
Chrome DevTools 111
community picks 111
Sublime Text 111
Yeoman 112
directory setup 76
directory structure 43, 44
Distributed Version Control System
 (DVCS) 11
Don't Repeat Yourself (DRY) 9

E

echo command 76
Eloquent JavaScript 109
errorCount function 57
expand 53
expect function 102
exports 32
ext 53
external tasks 103, 104

F

files 60
files, configuring
 about 49
 source directory, mapping to destination
  directory 52
 source files, multiple set 51
 source files, single set 51
filesSrc 60
File Transfer Protocol (FTP) 23-25
flags function 56
flatten 53
foo task 12, 65
fs.appendFileSync method 56

G

Git 11
GitHub 11
GitHub Gist 38
globbing 49
Grunt
 about 7
 benefits 10-13
 Command line interface (CLI) 37

continuous integration (CI) 103
deployment 23
features 9
Gruntfile.js file, example 8
installation 29
plugins 104-108
project, setting up 38
testing with 101-103
uglify plugin 8
use cases 13-17
grunt-cli module 37, 38
grunt-concurrent plugin 109
grunt.config function 45
grunt.config.get function 45, 54
grunt-contrib- 72
grunt-contrib-uglify plugin 43
grunt-contrib-watch plugin 96
grunt.current.task object 56
grunt.current.task property 60
Grunt, deployment
 about 23
 File Transfer Protocol (FTP) 23-25
 Secure File Transfer Protocol (SFTP) 25, 26
 Simple Storage Service (S3) 27, 28
grunt.fail.fatal function 47
grunt.fail.warn function 47
Gruntfile.js file 42, 43, 104
grunt --help command 67
grunt.initConfig function 45
grunt.loadNpmTasks function 104
grunt-mocha 102
grunt object 43
grunt.option function 66, 67
grunt.registerTask 55
grunt.template.process function 54
gzip compression 99

H

Haml 20
homepage property 106

I

Immediately-Invoked Function Expression
 (IIFE) 83
info grunt-gswg command 108
initConfig 8

[116]

Input/Output (I/O) task 29
installation, Grunt
  about 29
  modules 31-33
  Node.js 29-31
  npm 33
it function 102

J

Jade 17, 18
Jasmine 102
JavaScript
  resources 109, 110
JavaScript Object Notation (JSON) 39
JSHint 14
jshint task 15
JSLint 13

K

knox npm module 74

L

LESS 20
license property 106
Linting 13-15
LiveReload 96
LiveReload Chrome extension 96
load-grunt-tasks plugin 109
loadNpmTasks 8
loadNpmTasks function 104
loadTasks 105

M

Mac OSX 110
Make build tool 8
minification 20, 21
Mocha 102
module 32
module.exports object 43
modules
  about 31-34
  finding 35
  installing 36, 37
Mozilla Developer Network 109

multitasks
  about 58-61
  configuring 47, 48
multitasks, objects
  data 60
  files 60
  fileSrc 60
  target 60

N

nameArgs function 56
name function 56
Node.js
  about 8, 29-31
  installing 30, 31
node_modules directory 106
Node Package Manager. *See* npm
npm
  about 33, 34
  Frequently Asked Questions (FAQ) page 33
  modules, finding 35
  modules, installing 35-37

O

optimize option 66
options
  configuring 48, 49
options function 57, 61
options object 48

P

package 33
package.json file 39-41
Package.json Validator tool 42
peerDependencies property 108
PhantomJS 102
plugins
  about 104-107
  grunt-concurrent plugin 109
  load-grunt-tasks plugin 109

Q

Quality assurance (QA) team 98

R

rename 53
require function 32-34
requiresConfig function 56
requires function 56

S

Sass 20
Secure File Transfer Protocol (SFTP) 25, 26
Semantic Versioning Specification (SemVer) 39
Simple Storage Service (S3) 27, 28, 97
source files
 organizing 81
 scripts 81-83
 styles 87, 88
 views 85-87
SourceTree 111
src 53
src property 50
standard out (stdout) 76
static analysis 13-15
string property 47
Stylus 19
Sublime Text 111

T

target 60
task object, properties
 args function 56
 async function 56
 errorCount function 57
 flags function 56
 nameArgs function 56
 name function 56
 options function 57
 requiresConfig function 56
 requires function 56
task runner 7
tasks
 about 55
 aliasing 57, 58
 configuring 44-47
 files, configuring 49

multitasks, configuring 47, 48
 object 56
 options, configuring 48
 running 62
 templates 53
tasks, running
 automatically 70, 71
 command line 62, 63
 programmatically 69
templates 53, 54
third-party tasks
 about 72
 features 73, 74
 official versus user tasks 72
 popularity 73
 searching for 72
 stars 74
this.files array 59
this operator 57
transcompilation 16

U

uglify plugin 8
use cases
 about 13
 CoffeeScript 16, 17
 static analysis 13-15
 transcompilation 16

V

Version Control System (VCS) 44

W

watch task 70
WebStorm 111
WordPress 75

X

XMLHTTPRequest (XHR) 87

Y

Yeoman 112

[PACKT] open source*
PUBLISHING
community experience distilled

Thank you for buying
Getting Started with Grunt: The JavaScript Task Runner

About Packt Publishing

Packt, pronounced 'packed', published its first book "*Mastering phpMyAdmin for Effective MySQL Management*" in April 2004 and subsequently continued to specialize in publishing highly focused books on specific technologies and solutions.

Our books and publications share the experiences of your fellow IT professionals in adapting and customizing today's systems, applications, and frameworks. Our solution based books give you the knowledge and power to customize the software and technologies you're using to get the job done. Packt books are more specific and less general than the IT books you have seen in the past. Our unique business model allows us to bring you more focused information, giving you more of what you need to know, and less of what you don't.

Packt is a modern, yet unique publishing company, which focuses on producing quality, cutting-edge books for communities of developers, administrators, and newbies alike. For more information, please visit our website: `www.packtpub.com`.

About Packt Open Source

In 2010, Packt launched two new brands, Packt Open Source and Packt Enterprise, in order to continue its focus on specialization. This book is part of the Packt Open Source brand, home to books published on software built around Open Source license, and offering information to anybody from advanced developers to budding web designers. The Open Source brand also runs Packt's Open Source Royalty Scheme, by which Packt gives a royalty to each Open Source project about whose software a book is sold.

Writing for Packt

We welcome all inquiries from people who are interested in authoring. Book proposals should be sent to `author@packtpub.com`. If your book idea is still at an early stage and you would like to discuss it first before writing a formal book proposal, contact us; one of our commissioning editors will get in touch with you.

We're not just looking for published authors; if you have strong technical skills but no writing experience, our experienced editors can help you develop a writing career, or simply get some additional reward for your expertise.

[PACKT] open source
PUBLISHING
community experience distilled

Instant Testing with QUnit

ISBN: 978-1-78328-217-3 Paperback: 64 pages

Employ QUnit to increase your efficiency when testing JavaScript code

1. Learn something new in an Instant! A short, fast, focused guide delivering immediate results
2. Learn about cross-browser testing with QUnit
3. Learn how to use popular QUnit plugins and develop your own plugins
4. Hands-on examples on all the essential QUnit methods

JavaScript Testing Beginner's Guide

ISBN: 978-1-84951-000-4 Paperback: 272 pages

Test and debug JavaScript the easy way

1. Learn different techniques to test JavaScript, no matter how long or short your code might be
2. Discover the most important and free tools to help make your debugging task less painful
3. Discover how to test user interfaces that are controlled by JavaScript
4. Make use of free built-in browser features to quickly find out why your JavaScript code is not working, and most importantly, how to debug it

Please check **www.PacktPub.com** for information on our titles

[PACKT] open source
community experience distilled

PUBLISHING

Chef Infrastructure Automation Cookbook

ISBN: 978-1-84951-922-9　　　Paperback: 276 pages

Over 80 delicious recipes to automate your cloud and server infrastructure with Chef

1. Configure, deploy, and scale your applications
2. Automate error prone and tedious manual tasks
3. Manage your servers on-site or in the cloud
4. Solve real world automation challenges with task-based recipes
5. The book is filled with working code and easy-to-follow, step-by-step instructions

Object-Oriented JavaScript
Second Edition

ISBN: 978-1-84969-312-7　　　Paperback: 382 pages

Learn everything you need to know about OOJS in this comprehensive guide

1. Think in JavaScript
2. Make object-oriented programming accessible and understandable to web developers
3. Apply design patterns to solve JavaScript coding problems
4. Learn coding patterns that unleash the unique power of the language
5. Write better and more maintainable JavaScript code

Please check **www.PacktPub.com** for information on our titles

Printed in Great Britain
by Amazon.co.uk, Ltd.,
Marston Gate.